Introdu

The Talyllyn Railway's history is in Eglwys (Walk 18), where slate qua point 300 men removing 300,000 ton first, transported to Aberdyfi for shipment b a more efficient method was soon needed. In 1863 the quarry was leased to a group of mill owners, seeking to diversify as cotton supplies were becoming difficult to obtain. Engineer James Swinton Spooner, who had upgraded the Ffestiniog Railway to steam operation, was commissioned as engineer to construct a narrow-gauge line to connect with the new coastal railway.

After some initial difficulties, the Talyllyn Railway Company was formed, obtaining an Act of Parliament in 1865, and the line was built as far as Abergynolwyn, including provision for passenger services. Lines and inclines continued to the quarry further up the valley, although these extensions were never used for passenger traffic.

The Board of Trade Inspector, Captain Henry Tyler, finally approved the railway at the end of 1866. Clearances, as built, were very tight through the over-bridges, a problem which was overcome by sealing the carriage doors on the south side permanently shut, a feature which persists to this day.

Two steam engines, built by Fletcher Jennings of Whitehaven, provided the motive power, with three carriages and a guard's van being supplied by Brown Marshalls, and one by The Lancaster Carriage & Wagon Company. It is a tribute to their construction that these survived until 1951 and are still in daily use.

During the late 1800s the quarry and railway experienced problems, were offered for sale and purchased by William McConnel. They flourished for a while, but things finally came to a halt in 1909. Machinery was dismantled and the remaining slate stock sent down to Tywyn. In 1911 local MP Henry Haydn Jones bought the whole undertaking, but after a brief revival the quarry finally succumbed following a tunnel collapse in 1946.

The Talyllyn Railway Preservation Society was formed by a group of enthusiasts in 1950, following the death of Sir Haydn Jones, who had vowed to keep the railway open during his lifetime. In 1951 the Talyllyn Railway Preservation Society were handed the railway by Sir Haydn's widow. The first public trains to Rhydyronen ran on 14th of May 1952, with two trains Monday to Friday to Abergynolwyn starting on the 4th of June. The Nant Gwernol extension was opened in 1976 by Wynford Vaughan Thomas, following legal work by member George Tibbits.

All the walks in this guide are based around the railway – starting from the stations, which can be reached from Tywyn, and in one case also using a local bus service. Make sure you wear suitable footwear, carry a waterproof jacket and take some light refreshments. These can be obtained from the Railway's excellent cafés at Wharf Station or Abergynolwyn. Don't venture into any of the remaining quarry workings.

Have a great time using The Talyllyn Railway and exploring one of mid-Wales' most beautiful valleys.

WALK 1
PENDRE STATION WALK

DESCRIPTION An easy, level walk which visits St Cadfan's church before making a bee-line for the Afon Dysynni. After a walk beside the river, you turn inland, passing a fine dovecot and what remains of Ynysymaengwyn, once a stately home. A short walk along the road brings you to the ancient Croes-faen, where you turn left to either return to the start along quiet lanes, or make a short diversion to Hendy Station and a ride back on the train. The walk is less than 4 miles. You can return via Hendy Station, if you wish. Allow about 2½ hours.
START Pendre Station.

1 Leave Pendre Station and turn LEFT. At the cross roads turn RIGHT along Brook Street. When you reach the main road turn LEFT, passing the Corbett Arms Hotel and the cinema on your right. Turn RIGHT along Gwalia Road, after visiting the church of St Cadfan. Follow the road, which bends to the right, becomes a single track and continues across flat reclaimed land. Continue ahead when the tarmac ends and the view along the valley begins to open. Gradually the prominent dark outcrop of Birds' Rock comes into view on your right.

2 Go through a gate and continue. When paths cross, with a bridge to the left, ignore the sign pointing half-left and carry on for about 50 yards to pick up a faint path on top of a low embankment on the RIGHT. Walk along this to go through a gateway (no gate) and carry on heading for a very prominent direction sign ahead. Turn RIGHT to walk with the water to your left. *This is a popular area for local anglers.* You reach a stile by a gate.

3 Cross this stile and turn RIGHT over a footbridge. Go through a metal gate and follow the track, initially beside woods, and later beside a wall. Cross two little wooden footbridges, turn RIGHT and continue ahead along the path, surrounded by bluebells and wild garlic in the spring. Ignore paths off to the right to come to junction with a post with several waymarks where you turn LEFT to pass the 200-year old Evergreen Oak on the left. *Also known as the Holly Oak or Holm Oak, this is a Mediterranean native which was imported into the UK by Thomas Balle in the 18thC. The first trees were grown in Mamhead Park, Devon.* By the second picnic bench on the left turn RIGHT to descend a short flight of tiny stone steps. You pass a handsome dovecot (you can explore inside), one of the few remaining intact buildings of Ynysymaengwyn. Beside this are the former kennels. Turn LEFT opposite the dovecot and go ahead, then through a gateway on the RIGHT, followed by a second gateway to pass a small car park on the right. Beside this is a fine adventure playground, with a junior version close by. *The site of the old Ynysmaengwyn hall is here, but there is nothing left to see.* Follow the tarmac track around to the right, soon beside a caravan park. Finally you go through elaborate metal gates to reach the road *(note the elephant motif on gate-posts – the badge of the Corbett family).*

4 Turn RIGHT, cross the road and walk along the verge, TAKING GREAT CARE on this main road. Continue along the road until you reach a LEFT turn. Follow this, stopping to look at Croes-faen, the Dragon Stone just over the hedge. *This was once a marker on an ancient Pilgrim's Way: in legend it was placed here to protect the town from a ferocious dragon!* Turn LEFT at the next junction and continue. (If you wish, you can turn left again to reach Hendy Station, for a train ride back.) Cross the Talyllyn Railway and continue. When you reach the entrance to Ty-Mawr, turn RIGHT beside a handsome, but now redundant, step-stile, and walk along the track. Continue to return to Pendre Station.

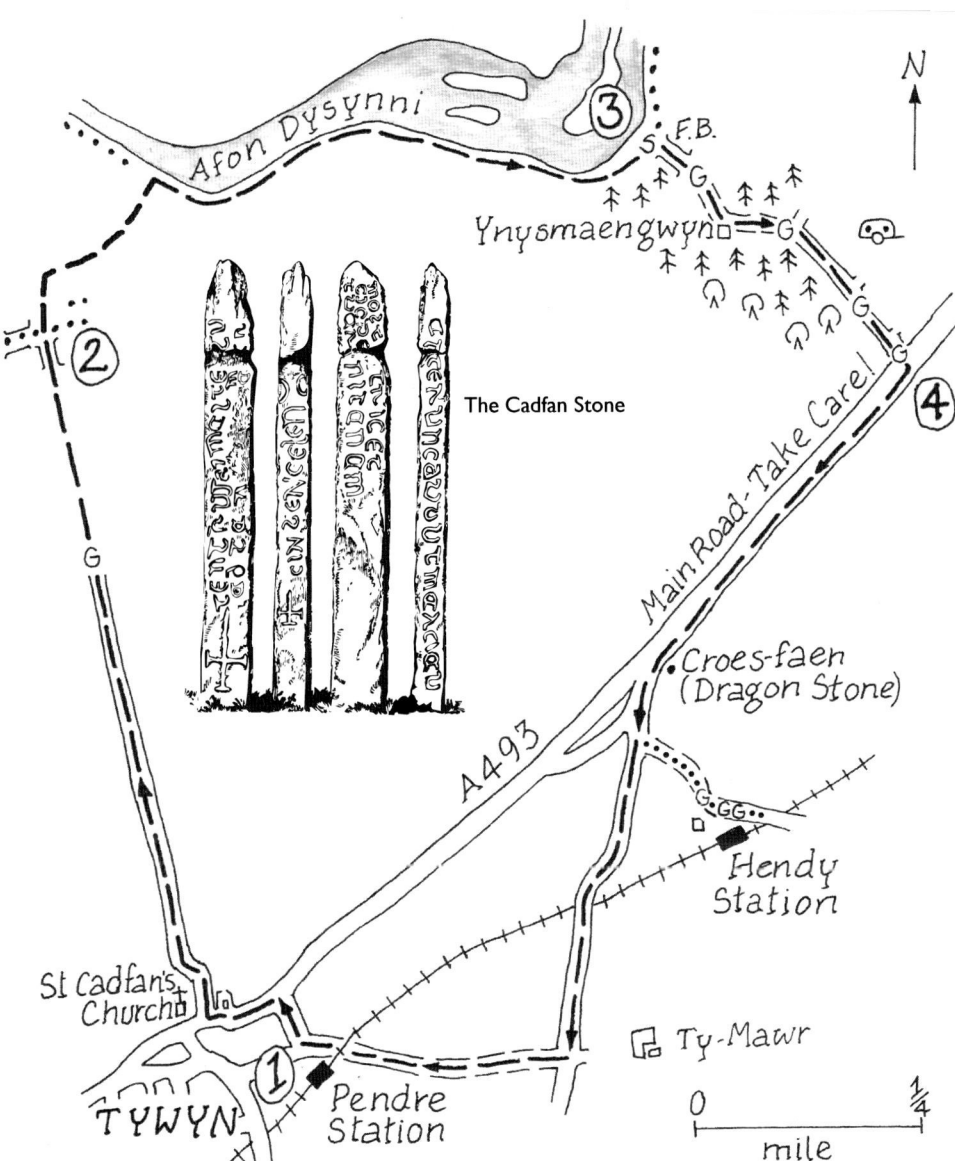

The Cadfan Stone

A couple of hundred yards north-west of the present St Cadfan's Church, under the floor of a garage, there is an ancient well. It was close to this, in the 6thC, that Cadfan arrived from Llanilltyd Fawr to found a school, and follow a simple life of study, hospitality and prayer. This was part of the general growth of the Celtic church during the latter part of the Roman occupation of Britain, and the years which followed. It is worth going inside the church to see the Cadfan Stone: on its four faces are inscriptions in what is considered to be some of the oldest written Welsh, proving that the leading families of the time used their native language, and not Latin.

WALK 2
BROAD WATER

DESCRIPTION Having walked along Tywyn's Main Street, passing cafés, pubs and shops, and perhaps stopping off at the church to explore (open daily 08.00-17.30). You then walk north across grassland, flat enough to land aeroplanes and, although there is little evidence left now, it was indeed a Second Word War aerodrome. Views are expansive, with the sea beyond defences to your left, and dramatic hills ahead and to your right. A short stretch beside the Afon Dysynni brings you to Broad Water, a fine expanse at high tide. Skirting a boggy area, you turn left to begin the return to Tywyn. Passing a World War II defence installation and shelter, built into the grass, you follow a rough road towards new houses. A short stretch beside the railway reaches a level crossing, which you cross and continue to a sea-side walkway. Soon you are back in Tywyn. 4¾ very level miles. Allow 2½ hours.
START Wharf Station, Tywyn.

1 From Wharf Station walk to the A493, Station Road, and turn left to continue towards the town centre, passing Tywyn Station. The road turns sharply right by the railway bridge, and continues as the High Street. Keep to the left and head towards St Cadfan's church. Pass the church and turn LEFT by the Magic Lantern cinema into Ffordd Gwalia, which swings left and then right and soon leaves the buildings behind as a great view opens to the north. Look out for the distinctive profile of Birds' Rock inland. Continue straight ahead beside drainage channels.

2 Go through a gate and continue. When paths cross, with a bridge to the left, ignore the sign pointing half-left and carry on for about 50 yards to pick up a faint path on top of a low embankment on the RIGHT. Walk along this to go through a gateway (no gate) and carry on heading for a very prominent direction sign ahead. Turn LEFT to follow the embankment beside the river.

3 The path curves around to the left as it reaches Broad Water and continues on the embankment, soon turning sharply right, staying beside the water. Eventually the waters' edge shallows and moves away to the right. Carry on ahead along a very low embankment, enclosing a very marshy area on the left and running roughly parallel to the water on the right. Maintain your direction to walk away from the water and soon reach a wide path at a T junction. Turn LEFT to walk between gorse bushes towards the left-hand end of a fence.

4 Go through gates to cross a bridge over a drainage channel to reach a prominent waymark post. Continue ahead, passing an old wartime pillbox, observation post and bunker and carry on along a rough tarmac track with a drainage channel to the right. By some old concrete foundations the track crosses the course of the channel and reaches houses. Turn RIGHT, go through a gate and carry on to reach a road.

5 Turn LEFT and walk along this minor road, with the railway on the right. When the road swings to the left you reach a level crossing on the right. Turn RIGHT here, cross the railway and walk by Bryn y Mor Caravan & Camping park. Go through a gate at the end and then down steps to reach the promenade by the sea. Turn LEFT to walk beside the beach.

6 The footway swings LEFT. Carry on inland along the road, staying on the left hand side to eventually pass under the railway bridge, where you turn RIGHT to return to Wharf Station along Station Road.

St Cadfan's Church
It was in the 6thC that Cadfan arrived from Llanilltyd Fawr. At that time Cadfan's church was built of wood, and was easily destroyed during Viking raids. It was decided to construct a more substantial building during the mid-12thC. Around this building a town slowly grew, and a shipping trade built up. It is worth going inside to see the Cadfan Stone and fine medieval stone carvings: one, known as the Crying Knight, 'weeps' during

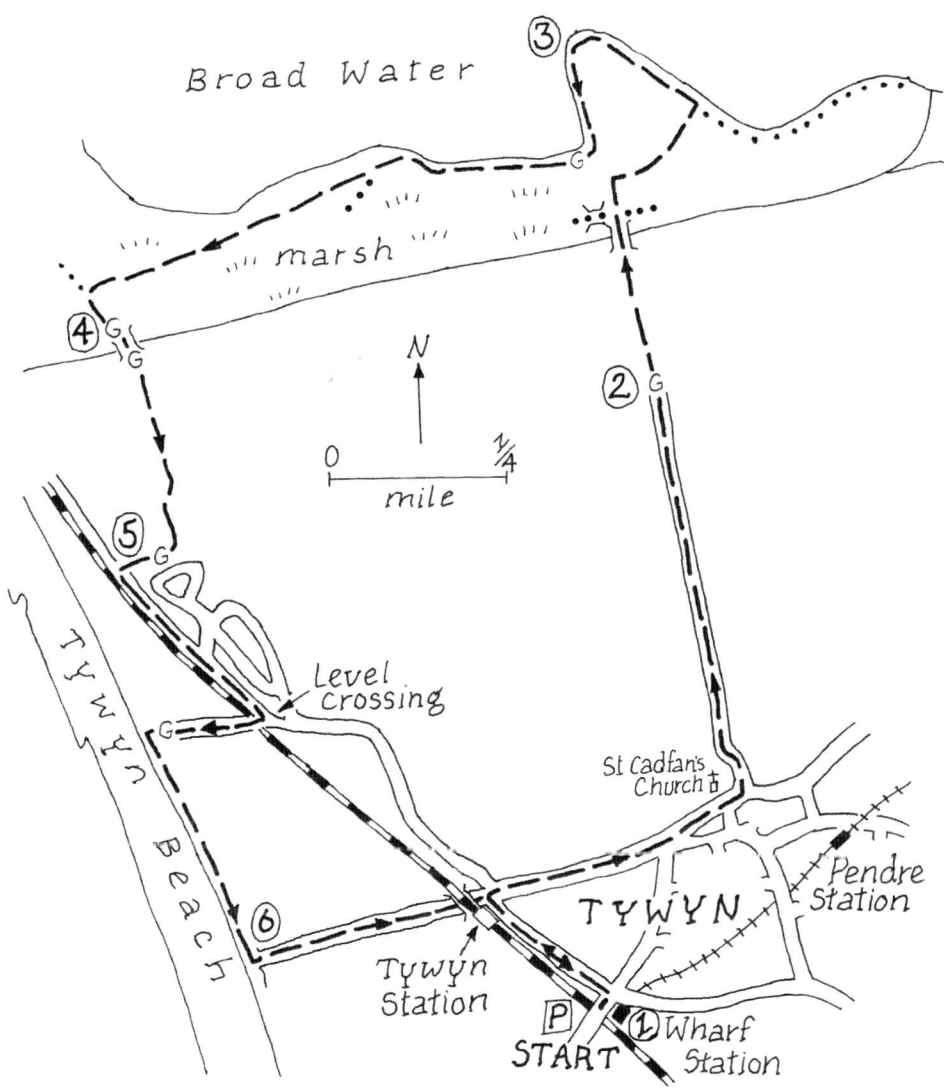

wet weather. A new tower was constructed in 1736, but it was taken down around 1880 when the vicar, the Rev. Titus Lewis, had a vision to rebuild the church as it once was. With financial assistance from some rich local families, including the Corbetts, he realised his dream, rebuilding the tower in its original central position.

In the 16thC, during the reformation, a vicar from St Cadfan's went to London to campaign against changes being introduced from Europe (sounds familiar!) and was, for his trouble, hung, drawn and quartered. A time of hardship followed the Civil War, and a general lack of cash for maintenance led to the collapse, in 1692, of the church tower. This buried both the altar and a 13thC sanctus bell, which was not recovered until 1881.

The church is open daily.

WALK 3
RHYDYRONEN TO PENDRE

DESCRIPTION From the station at Rhydyronen there is a splendid easy walk beside the railway to Hendy Station, and then mainly by quiet roads to Pendre Station for a brief train ride back to Tywyn. The total distance is about 1½ miles. Allow about an hour.
START Rhydyronen Station.

gateway, ahead but a short distance away from the railway line. Go through and continue ahead to reach yet another gate. Continue to go through the gate, veer to the right and go through another gate.

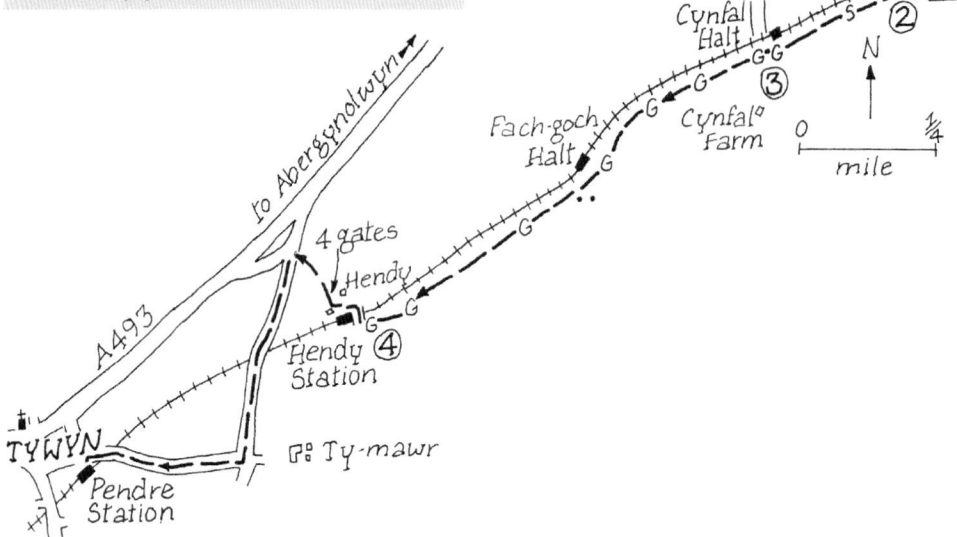

1 Take the Talyllyn Railway to Rhydyronen Station. From here walk to the road, turn right and cross over the railway bridge.

2 Cross the tall ladder stile on your RIGHT and walk with the railway line on your right. Cross a stile beside a gate and continue ahead.

3 Go through a gate, cross a lane and go through another gate and continue ahead. Pass through three more gates beside the railway, then look out for another waymarked

4 Cross the bridge over the railway. Now ignore a metal field gate to your right but walk ahead for a few strides, and then go through the wooden gate to the RIGHT to walk through the farmyard at Hendy, veering right and passing through another four gates before you leave the farm and walk along a tarmac driveway to reach the road. Turn LEFT. Walk along the lane, cross over the railway and continue until you reach Ty-mawr on the left. Now turn RIGHT beside a sturdy, but disused, stone stile and walk along a single-track tarmac lane which widens as it reaches houses at the edge of Tywyn. Continue ahead to cross a level crossing at Pendre Station to rejoin the Talyllyn Railway.

WALK 4
RHYDYRONEN & BRAICH-Y-RHIW

DESCRIPTION From the station at Rhydyronen there is an excellent walk up the steep-sided valley of Nant Braich-y-rhiw. After passing Braich-y-rhiw and crossing a series of gates and a stile, you turn sharp left shortly after crossing a bridge for a straightforward return to the start.
START Rydyronen Station.

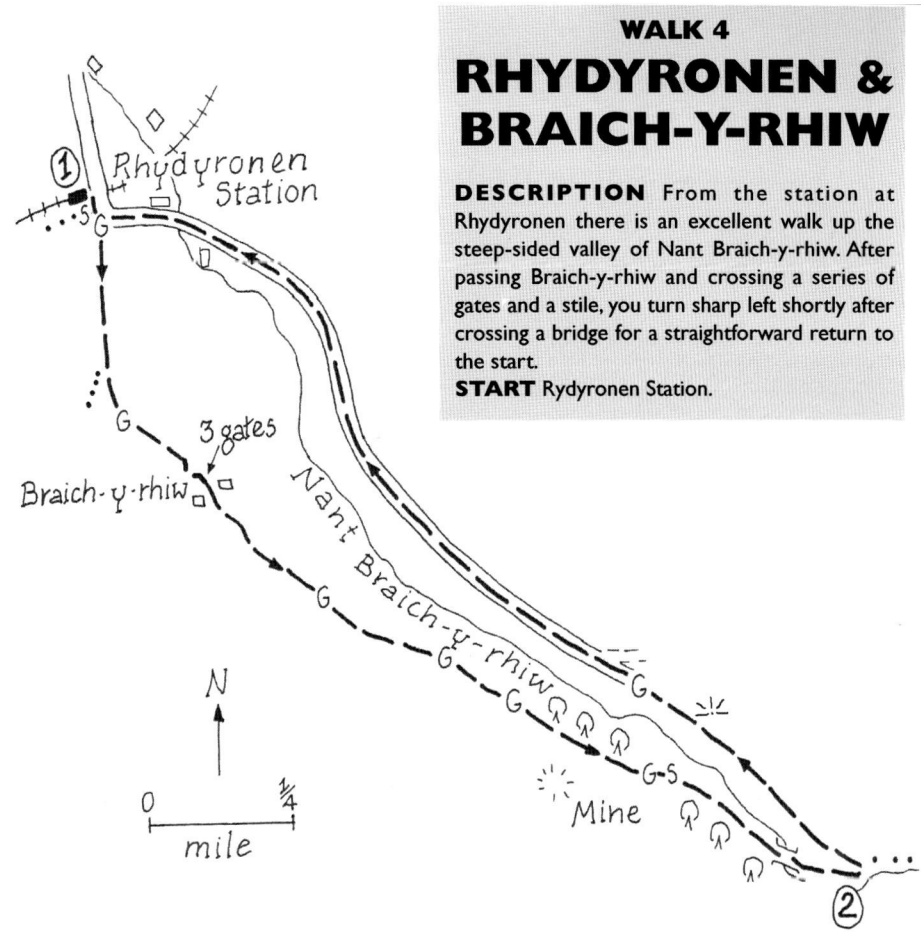

1 Take the Talyllyn Railway to Rhydyronen Station. From the station walk to the road, turn right and cross over the railway bridge. Go through a gate and walk ahead along a waymarked lane, which soon forks. Walk to the LEFT, go through the gate ahead and walk up to Braich-y-rhiw. Go through the right-hand gate and walk by the farmhouse, going through two more gates and leaving by a very handsome, but ruinous, barn. Now continue ahead along a track, keeping a fence to your left. Go through a gate, and continue ahead. Go through another gate, and carry on, with trees to your left, and old mine workings up to the right. Pass through a gate and then climb a stile beside an old ffridd, or livestock pen. Now veer LEFT diagonally down towards the stream. Cross the narrow bridge and continue ahead, climbing the bank to reach a lane.

2 Turn sharp LEFT and walk back down the lane, going through a gate and enjoying the expansive views ahead. After passing a small terrace of cottages on your right, follow the road to return to the station.

WALK 5
RHYDYRONEN & DYSYNNI

DESCRIPTION Following quiet lanes and pretty riverside paths down to the Afon Dysynni, this is an easy walk which offers expansive views towards the sea in the west, and the mountains to the east. Your return route passes Ynysymaengwyn on its way back to the station. It is about 4 miles, so allow 2½ hours.
START Rhydyronen Station.

1 Leave the Rhydyronen station, walk to the road and turn LEFT. Pass the entrance to Tynllwyn Farm Caravan Park on the right. When you reach a footpath sign by a stone step-stile on the right, turn RIGHT, cross the stile, and the footbridge immediately after, and turn LEFT, to walk beside Nant Rhydyronen. Go through a gate and continue beside the stream. When you reach a gate tucked away in the corner, go through and turn RIGHT. Walk with the hedge to your right to eventually reach a gate beside factory buildings. Go through this and continue to reach the road, and then turn LEFT.

2 After a few yards you reach a main road. Cross this and follow the lane directly ahead. When you reach a kissing gate by a house, go through and follow the lane, crossing a small bridge. Pass a white house on the left and continue along a path, with a wooden fence on your left. Keep walking ahead to reach a stile to the left, ignoring a stile on the right. Follow the path behind houses to reach a road, where you turn RIGHT. Walk to a road junction, noting a kissing gate and footpath sign on the left. You will return to this. At the road junction, on a small enclosure to the left is an old pump. Facing this across the road is the Peniarth Arms (food, accommodation, real ale. Tel: 01654 288096).

3 Return to the kissing gate and go through. Walk with the river to your right. Go through a gate and continue beside the river to a gate, which you go through. continue to go through two gates. When you reach the Dysynni, turn LEFT through a gate, to walk with the river to your right. *The views north-east towards Birds' Rock are splendid.*

4 Walk beside the river, ignoring the first waymark post you reach, and continue towards trees ahead. Go through a gate and continue.

5 Turn LEFT to cross two little wooden footbridges. Follow the path, passing the fine dovecot and stables of what was once Ynysymaengwyn. Climb some steps and follow the path by the evergreen oak. Carry on ahead, then turn RIGHT to reach the car park and curve to the right, passing the site of the old mansion on the right, and following the lane beside the caravan park. Leave the park through metal gates. Carefully cross the road and turn LEFT, to walk along the road. Continue, passing the house and farm buildings of Ysguboriau.

6 When you reach a waymarked gate in the hedge, turn RIGHT, go through and walk with a hedge and fence on your right. Cut across the field corner to head for a ladder stile to the left of Cil-y-Parc. Cross this and continue ahead, soon joining the track which leads to the house. Cross the stile by the gate, join the road and turn RIGHT.

7 Continue along the road to reach Cynfal Halt. To return to Rhydyronen Station turn LEFT after the bridge and follow the path by the railway to reach the staion.

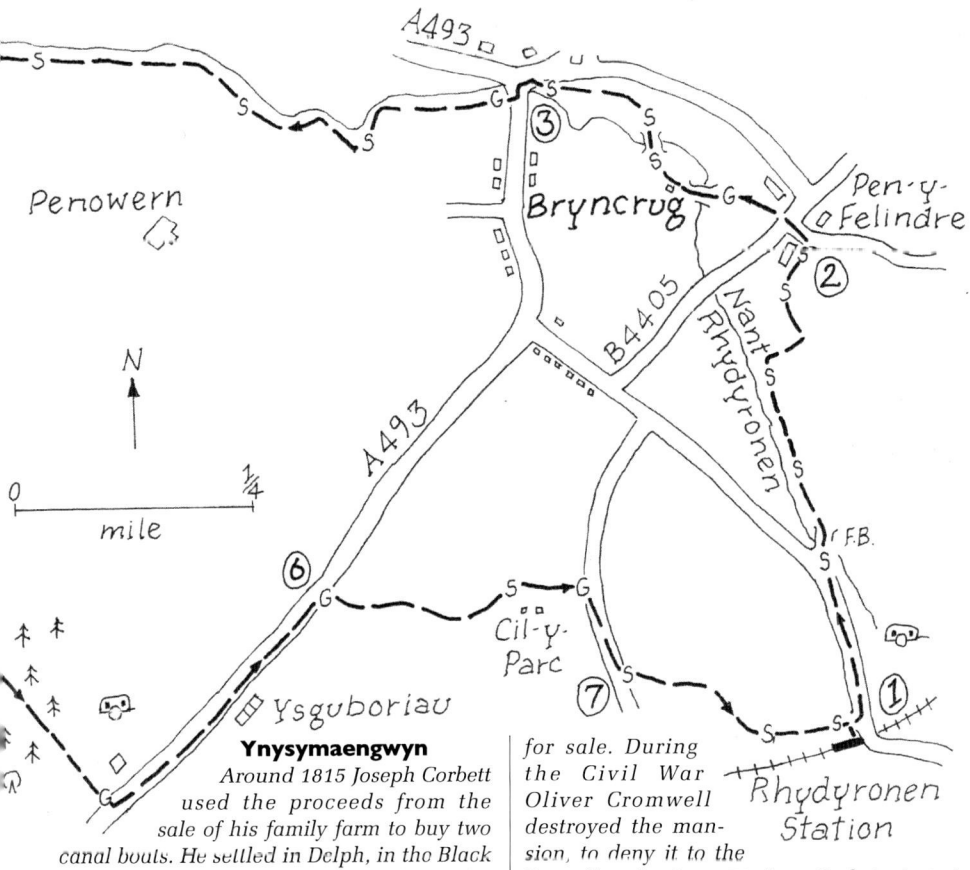

Ynysymaengwyn

Around 1815 Joseph Corbett used the proceeds from the sale of his family farm to buy two canal boats. He settled in Delph, in the Black Country, where his wife gave birth to John in 1817. The boats carried iron from the Leys Ironworks, and it was at the works that John was apprenticed in 1840. He realised that, with the coming of the railways, the canal business would go into decline. So they sold up and John found a new investment at Stoke Prior, where the ailing British Alkali had found huge deposits of salt. Purchasing the company for £1035 18s 9d, John modernised production and improved his employees' conditions. In 1880 he sold the works for £660,000.

With his vivacious wife Anna, he purchased the Manor of Impney, but his new wife's allegiance to the Catholic church led to a rift in their relationship. In 1874 John became Liberal MP for Droitwich. An acquaintance of John Corbett mentioned that Ynysymaengwyn, near Tywyn, was up for sale. During the Civil War Oliver Cromwell destroyed the mansion, to deny it to the Roundheads. In 1758 Ann Corbet started building a mansion. She also built the dovecot, which is virtually all that now remains of this great venture. Ann's successors gradually frittered away their inheritance, and the house was eventually sold to John Corbett, who undertook an enthusiastic restoration. Following his death in 1901 his wife Anna, and the children, came to live at Ynysymaengwyn, and she cared for it until her death in 1914. In the expectation of a secure future for the estate, Mary Corbett gave it to Merioneth County Council, who in turn passed it to Tywyn Council in 1948.

In a sorry state of repair, it was burnt as an exercise for the local Fire Service, and flattened by the army. Now only the dovecot and a few ruined buildings remain. Look out for the elephant motifs on the gateposts – the badges of the Corbet (one 't') family.

WALK 6
RHYDYRONEN & BRYNGLAS

DESCRIPTION This route presents you with a choice of walks: station to station either way, or an enjoyable journey around the whole circuit. If you choose to start from Rhydyronen you are soon presented with a stunning vista of the sea and the valley as you climb gently up the lower slopes of the south-western extremities of the Tarrens. A steep descent brings you back to the railway at Brynglas Station, an alternative starting point. You then pass a fine converted mill and the handsome house of Dolau-gwyn before making your way through woods and beside Nant Rhydyronen back to the start. It is 1½miles from Rhydyronen Station via Tynllwyn-Hen to Brynglas Station, and a little over 2 miles for the return walk via Bryncrug, making a total circuit of less than 4 miles. Allow about 3 hours.
START Rhydyronen Station (or Brynglas Station).

1 Leave Rhydyronen Station and turn sharp RIGHT to cross the bridge over the railway line. Continue along the lane, which bends left and passes a fine water-pump on the right. Turn LEFT along the lane signed to 'Tynllwyn-Hen', and soon ford a small stream. Fine views open up to your left. Pass a house on the left and walk towards 'Tynllwyn-Hen'. As you approach 'Tynllwyn-Hen' turn SHARP RIGHT through a gap in a stone wall and then turn HALF-LEFT to walk uphill to a waymarked stile by a gate.

2 Cross this stile and turn RIGHT to walk along an old green lane, with a fence on the right. Go through a gate and turn LEFT to walk below the track but to the right of the fence. Pass a waymarked fence post on the left and go through a gate. Immediately turn LEFT and then RIGHT, to walk with the fence on your right. *There are splendid views ahead towards Cadair Idris.* Cross a stile and continue HALF-RIGHT, as the fence goes away to the right, to reach a stile. Cross this and maintain your direction to another stile. Cross this and veer uphill towards a large prominent rock. Pass this and continue to the wall, and then on to an opening by a sheep fold.

3 DO NOT go through this opening, but turn LEFT to walk steeply downhill to reach a stile beside a gate (by another gate in the wall). Cross the stile and continue downhill with a stone wall to the right. Cross the stile beside the gate ahead at the end of the wall, and walk HALF-RIGHT down the field to cross a stile by the railway. Go through gates on the RIGHT to emerge at Brynglas Station.

4 Turn LEFT, carefully cross the level crossing and continue along the lane. *Note the Ground Frame Hut on the left, which has a very fine token machine.* When the lane bends slightly left, turn RIGHT to go through a metal gate and continue to the next gate. Go through this, cross the bridge over Afon Fathew and continue, passing a converted mill. Go through the next gate and pass 'Dolau-gwyn' to emerge through a gate to reach a road. Turn LEFT and walk about 100 yards to a footpath sign on the right.

5 Turn RIGHT, cross the stile beside a gate and follow the path AHEAD and uphill. Climb steps and continue uphill and left as signed. You soon join a tarmac road. When this forks, go to the RIGHT, uphill. Carry on ahead, passing 'no 5', to a stile. Cross this and continue, enjoying the fine view ahead. You soon descend stone steps beside an old barn, and pass a 'helem' (Dutch barn) on your left to reach a track junction.

6 Walk to a waymarked gate ahead, go through and continue. Cross a ladder stile and carry on with a fence on the left. When you reach a ladder stile, turn LEFT, cross it and walk downhill with a fence to the right. When you have passed 'Braichyrhenllys' turn RIGHT as signed, then walk towards a waymark post, with the sea in the distance. Now veer LEFT down an old green lane to join a fence on the left. Cross a ladder stile and descend to the road. Turn LEFT to reach the main road, where you turn RIGHT.

WALK 6

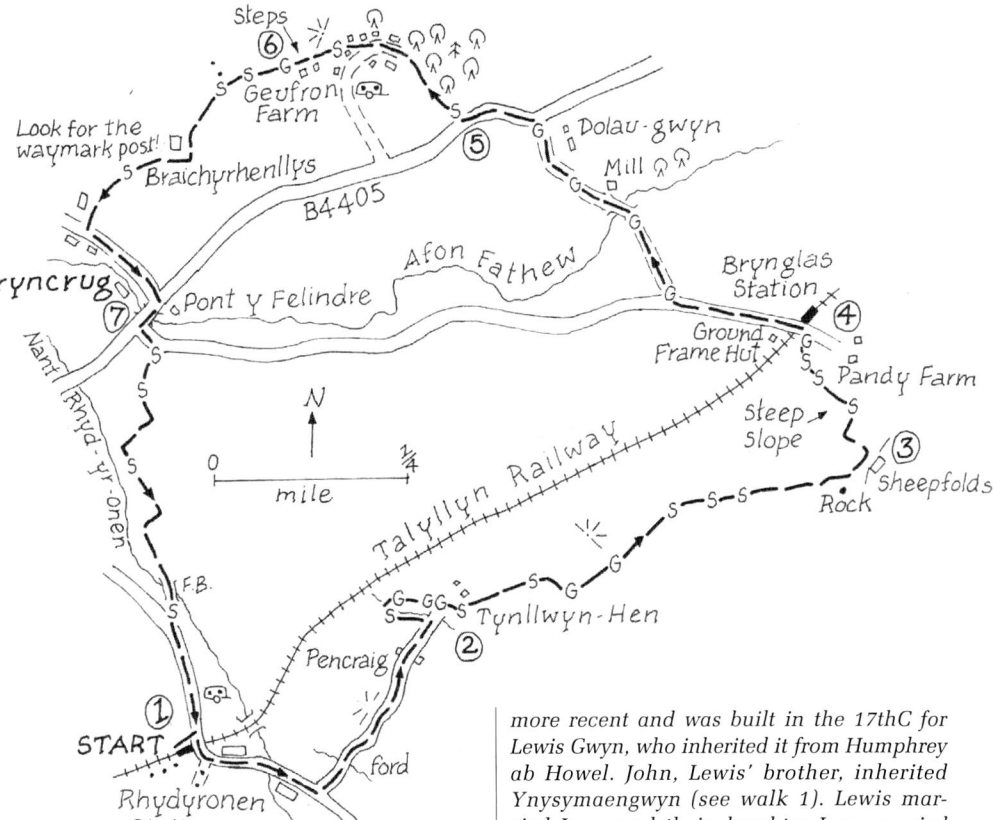

7 Cross the bridge and turn LEFT. Pass factory buildings on the right and, immediately after, turn RIGHT and cross a stile. Follow the path, cross a stile and walk with a hedge on the left. Continue beside the hedge when it bends to the right, to reach a stile. Turn LEFT, cross the stile and walk with a stream to the right. Cross the next stile and continue beside the stream. You then reach a footbridge, which you cross, and then a fine stone step-stile ahead. Cross this and turn LEFT to return to Rhydyronen Station.

Dolau-gwyn

Handsomely built, with crow-stepped gables and mullioned windows, Dolau-gwyn – meaning bright or white meadows – is one of the finest examples of a 17thC squire's house in Meirionydd. The estate dates from Norman times, but the house is more recent and was built in the 17thC for Lewis Gwyn, who inherited it from Humphrey ab Howel. John, Lewis' brother, inherited Ynysymaengwyn (see walk 1). Lewis married Jane, and their daughter Jane married Gruffydd Nannau: Dolau-gwyn remained in their family for over 250 years, until it was sold to John Silvester.

Many original features have been retained within the house: there is a fine plaster coat of arms dating from 1620 above the kitchen mantelpiece, with another in the drawing room dated 1656 – this room also has a splendid moulded plaster ceiling; the traditional Welsh kitchen has oak beams and settles, and each of the bedrooms has a moulded plaster coat of arms over the mantelpiece. Not being 'offered' food and shelter at Ynysymaengwyn, Oliver Cromwell is said to have burnt the house down to deny it to the Roundheads during the Civil War: he then stayed at Dolau-gwyn for one night when the then occupants thought better of denying him!

The house and grounds are now a private residence. They are NOT open to the public.

WALK 7
BIRDS' ROCK

DESCRIPTION Birds' Rock is a prominent landmark in Dyffryn Dysynni. On this walk you cross from the railway over hills to the very minor road which passes this famous and prominent craggy rock, an historic nesting site for cormorants, who still condduct their lives as if the sea still came up to the base of the cliff. You then climb around the southern side of the rock to make your return to the station. About 5 mlies, allow 3½ hours.
START Dolgoch Station.

1 From Dolgôch Station walk away from the falls, passing through the metal gate to reach the Dolgôch Falls Hotel. Pass this and join the main road by the car park. Carry straight on (towards Tywyn) and, when the road bends to the left, climb steps and cross the stile ahead. Turn LEFT. Now veer RIGHT up the field, ignoring a metal gate to your left. Carry on AHEAD when the fence on the left ends, climbing a rocky slope then crossing a field to a stile. Cross this and continue ahead. Look for a stile by a waymark post (to the right of a gate ahead), cross it and carry on, with a fence to your left (and mind the iris plants in spring). You reach a ladder stile. Cross this and a small stream, and continue as signed, with a fence on the left, to reach another stile. Cross this and turn RIGHT along a lane towards 'Ty-Mawr'.

2 Pass the farmhouse and, when the track forks, go LEFT through a gate and along a track. Keep to the track as it zig-zags uphill, and stop to enjoy splendid views south-west over the valley. Go through a gate and continue along the track. When you reach a gate by a waymark post, go through and stay on the track. Go through another gate by 'Bwlch-y-Maen'. Ignore a track to the right and continue AHEAD.

3 When the track turns sharp right, turn LEFT along a track. Cross a stile beside a gate and continue, following the line of an old track as it curves to the right. Then, when you reach an old gateway in a stone wall, turn LEFT and go through. Now turn RIGHT and continue. You pass a large stone on the left before reaching a gate. Go through this gate and continue along the green track. Go through a gate and continue with a fence, and then a wall, on your right. You descend to reach a road. When you see a ladder stile ahead, leave the track down steps to the right.

4 Cross the stile and turn LEFT. When the road forks, go LEFT to walk beside and below Birds' Rock. *Cormorants still nest here, a relic of a time when the sea level was higher, and the rock was on the coast.* As you leave the rocks behind you pass the entrance to Gesail. Now look out for a stile on your LEFT.

Birds' Rock

WALK 7

5 Cross this stile and walk up the field to join a track through the woods. This track climbs through the trees and then reaches the edge of the wood. Now veer LEFT, climbing more steeply up to a stile. Cross this and carry on, veering slightly LEFT around trees to reach a stile. Cross this and continue with a fence on the right. Continue past a ruined stone building on the left to where the track forks. Go LEFT uphill, then veer LEFT beside a fence to reach a stile. Cross this and continue AHEAD.

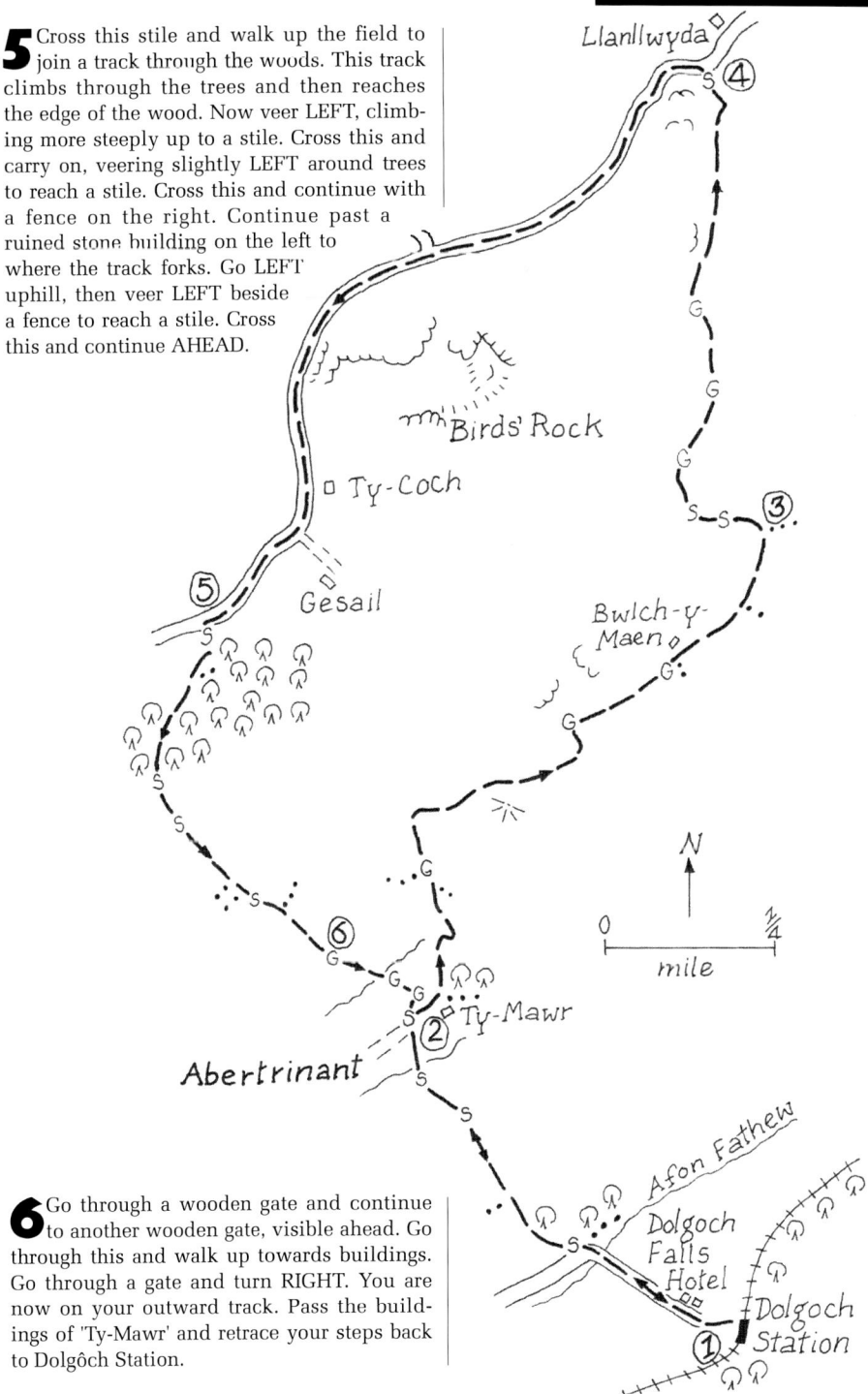

6 Go through a wooden gate and continue to another wooden gate, visible ahead. Go through this and walk up towards buildings. Go through a gate and turn RIGHT. You are now on your outward track. Pass the buildings of 'Ty-Mawr' and retrace your steps back to Dolgôch Station.

WALK 8
THE ABERTRINANT LOOP

DESCRIPTION A great route to explore from Dolgoch, taking you on a circuit through Abertrinant, giving you stunning views over the valley, where steam trains run up to the terminus at Nant Gwernol. There is quite a steep climb beyond Tan-y-coed-uchaf. This walk can also start from Quarry Siding Halt. From here, walk down to the main road and turn RIGHT. After a short distance, turn LEFT along the lane to Tan-y-coed-isaf. By the house, turn RIGHT along the waymarked track and follow the instructions from point 2 below. The total distance is about 3 miles. Allow about 2½ hours.
START Dolgoch Falls Station.

1 Walk away from Dolgoch Station towards the road. Go through a gate and turn left, then go through a second gate and walk along the lane beside the hotel and the car park to reach the road. Continue ahead, walking very carefully beside the road and, when the road bends to the left, climb up to the waymarked stile on the right, cross it and turn RIGHT. Follow the footpath, with a stream to your right. Go through a metal gate and continue ahead. Go through a gate into woods and carry on along the green track. Cross a ladder stile and continue to reach a gate. Go through, passing Tan-y-coed-isaf on your right, and continue. When the track bends to the right around the house, turn LEFT up a bank as waymarked.

2 Then go through a gate and continue along the green track. Ignore a gate on your right, by an electricity pole, and continue, walking gently uphill. When the path forks, go to the LEFT. Cross a stile by a gate and continue. Go through another gate and keep left, to follow the path behind Tan-y-coed-uchaf. Go through the gate above the farm and walk to a wooden gate. Go through and continue up to a path crossing.

3 Turn sharp LEFT, passing a rack of 'fire beaters' and continue along a green track. Go through a wooden gate and follow the track, which now starts climbing. *The views from here, across the valley, are excellent.* Cross a low fence – the stile is missing – and follow the path up and around the hillside to the right. The path then dips, and you can step across a stream. Now veer right and follow a narrow, climbing, path. Look for a ladder-stile hidden in the field corner. Cross it and turn LEFT, to walk with a fence to your left. When the fence becomes a wall and bears away to the left, continue AHEAD on a green track, in the direction of a distinct mountain summit ahead. Ignore the first obvious gate on the left and continue, with the fence on your left and crossing a marshy patch, to reach a metal gate, with a stile and a marker-post beside it. Cross the stile and walk downhill, gradually veering right to reach a waymarked stile by a gate. Cross it and walk with a fence on your right, continuing ahead and passing waymarked gates. Follow the path to go through the gate beside Ty-mawr.

4 Turn LEFT onto a tarmac lane and walk through the farm. *The old stone buildings here are extremely attractive, if a little run down.* Continue along the lane, looking for a waymarked stile on the LEFT, with a delightfully old-fashioned sign. Cross the stile and walk ahead to reach a ladder stile, in a boggy patch full of wild iris. Cross the stile and carry on ahead with the fence to your right. Cross a small waymarked stile in

WALK 8

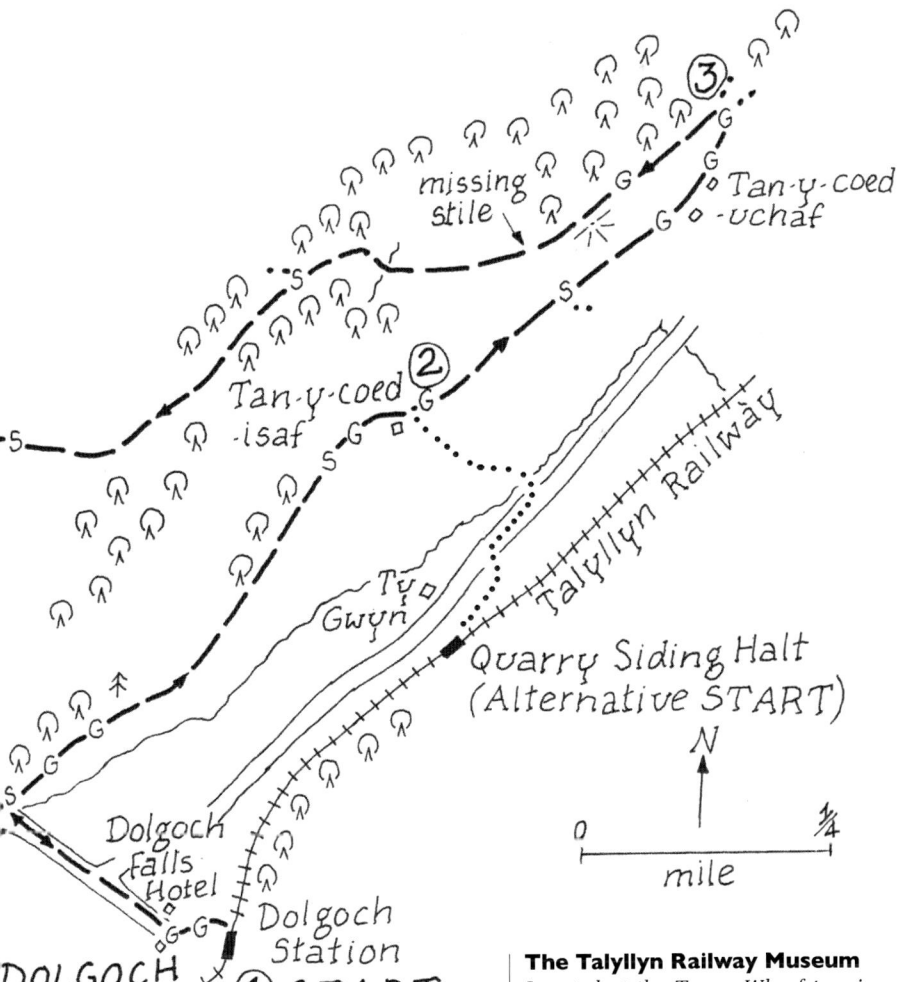

The Talyllyn Railway Museum

Located at the Tywyn Wharf terminus of the Talyllyn Railway, the Narrow Gauge Railway Museum has an important collection of artefacts relating to narrow gauge railways in the British Isles, throughout a period spanning some 200 years. The collection ranges from complete locomotives to smaller items such as paperwork, signalling equipment and tickets. It is a unique and comprehensive record of these fascinating railways, nearly 80 of which are represented in the collection. The Museum is well worth a visit, and is open from 09.30 – 17.00 daily from late March to the end of October, and during the Christmas and New Year holiday period.

the field corner and continue ahead, veering to the right of a hillock to reach a stile. Cross this and continue downhill, with a fence to your right. The route bends to the left as you approach the road, and a distinct path leads back to the ladder stile by the footpath sign. Cross this and walk carefully ahead along the road to return to Dolgoch Station.

WALK 9
THE DYSYNNI GORGE

DESCRIPTION After a short stretch of road, you are soon walking along a steep gorge defined by the Afon Dysynni, which squeezes through this narrow gap before reaching Dyffryn Dysynni, where it turns south-west and heads for the sea. A very quiet lane is then joined at Pont Ystumanner and this is followed for a short way to Llanllwyda, with the craggy hulk of Birds's Rock directly ahead. You then turn left to start your return, initially climbing steadily and then more steeply, amidst surroundings which seem remarkably remote. Your climb ends at Rhiwerfa, where you turn left and begin a fairly steep descent through woods and down to the road. Opposite, just across the valley, is the Talyllyn Railway. You then return along the main road to Abergynolwyn Station. The total distance is about 5 miles. Allow about 4 hours.
START Abergynolwyn Station.

1 Leave Abergynolwyn Station and walk down to the road. Turn RIGHT and walk along the verge until you see a footpath sign on the LEFT-HAND side, as you are approaching Abergynolwyn. Carefully cross the road and walk up the track as directed for about 15 yards, cross a stile and follow the track to the RIGHT. Cross a ladder-stile by a gate and continue. Pass a house to the right as the clear track ends. Maintain your direction across a field towards a tiny section of fence over an equally small stream. Here the path becomes clearly defined – continue along the gorge, with the Dysynni to your right. Cross a ladder stile and continue, with the river now well below you on the right. The views here are superb. Cross a stile and continue, to reach another stile. Cross this and continue. Eventually the path descends and joins the river. Pass a gate and stile by a broken fence and keep to the path. Go through the RIGHT-HAND gate by Rhiwlas and then descend along the track to join a minor road through a gate.

2 Continue AHEAD along the road (DON'T cross the bridge), with the river still to your right. *Pass Tyn-y-bryn, the house of Dr William Owen Pugh 1759-1835.* Continue along the road, to eventually reach Llanllwyda, where there is excellent caravanning and camping (01654 782276). *The craggy profile of Birds' Rock is dead ahead.*

3 As the road bends to the right, turn LEFT over the signed ladder-stile and climb to join a green track, which continues uphill beside a stone wall on the left. Follow this up to a gate, go through and continue, curving initially to the left and then around the hill to the right. Go through a gate and continue ahead. Look for a gap in the wall to your LEFT. Go through this and continue ahead to

WALK 9

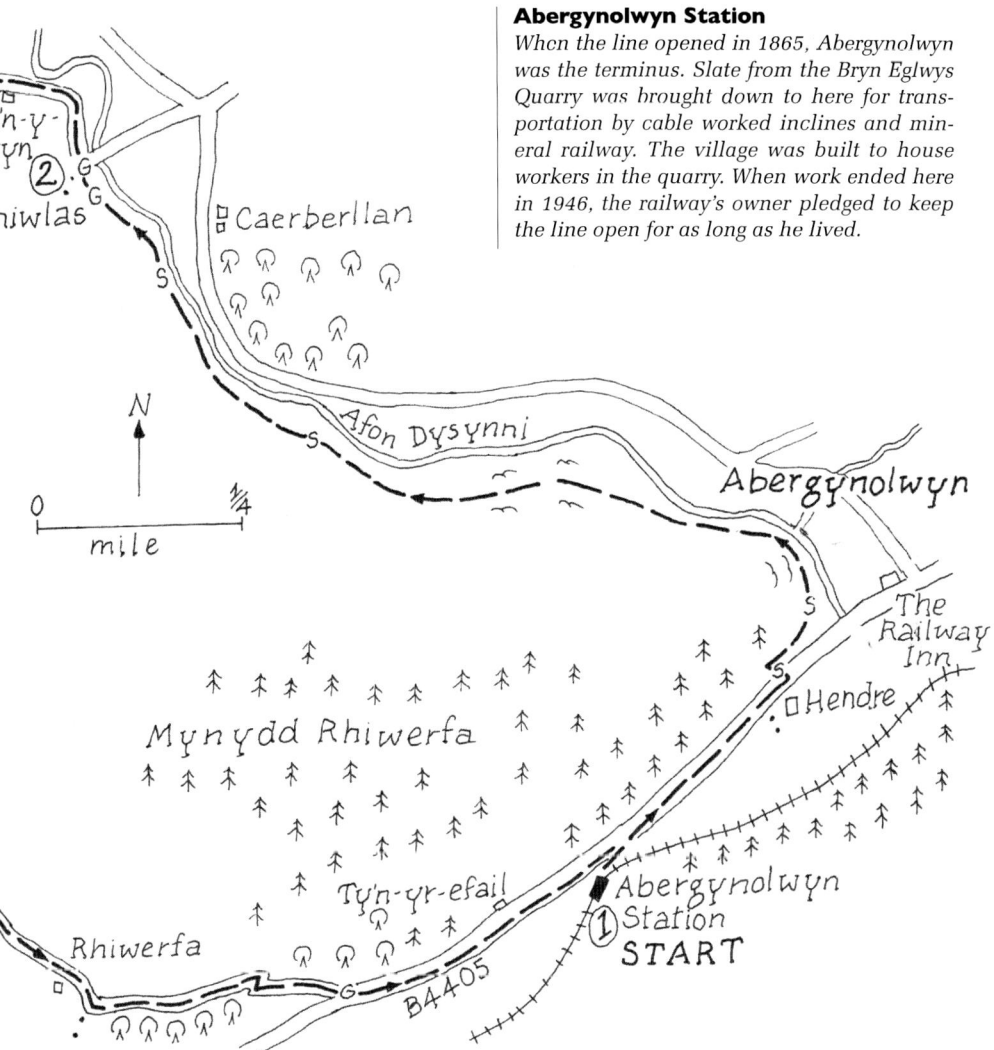

Abergynolwyn Station
When the line opened in 1865, Abergynolwyn was the terminus. Slate from the Bryn Eglwys Quarry was brought down to here for transportation by cable worked inclines and mineral railway. The village was built to house workers in the quarry. When work ended here in 1946, the railway's owner pledged to keep the line open for as long as he lived.

cross a stile by a gate. Now follow a track to join a surfaced lane.

4 Turn LEFT. Go through a gate and follow the surfaced lane, continuing through another gate and on beneath trees. Continue on the lane, passing Rhiwerfa. Ignore the footpath which beckons to the right and continue along the lane. Ignore the forest track on the left and continue downhill to descend a very steep 'S' bend, enjoying the views along the valley which open up as the trees clear. Join the main road through a gate, cross the road and turn LEFT to return to Abergynolwyn Station, walking along the wide grassy verge. Or you can reward yourself with either a pint and/or a meal at The Railway Inn (friendly, real ale, good food, 01654 782744) or a meal at the excellent and friendly Caffi'r Ceunant (01654 782372, 09.00-16.00, closed Tuesday) before returning to the station.

WALK 10
CASTELL Y BERE

DESCRIPTION A fascinating route which circumnavigates Foel Cae'rberllan and passes through the village of Abergynolwyn, where you can enjoy a drink and a meal at The Railway Inn or a visit to Caffi'r Ceunant. You then walk along a valley with the Afon Dysynni hemmed in at its base before veering off above Coed Cae'rberllan and approaching Castell y Bere, prominent on a rocky outcrop to your left. After visiting what is one of Wales' most romantic castles you then make your return along the cwm of Nant-yr-eira, initially through woods and then along an open trackway. You then drop down to the lane to make a level return to the village, where a path takes you beside the river. The total distance is around 5½ miles. Allow about 4 hours.

START Nant Gwernol Station

1 Leave the platform at the far end of the station, cross the footbridge and turn LEFT to walk downhill, with waterfalls to your left. When you join a lane, turn left and walk steeply downhill to Abergynolwyn. Cross the road and walk along the minor road to the right of The Railway Inn. Continue along Heol Llanegryn, passing single storey cottages on the left and climb the hill. At the road junction continue ahead as signed to Castell y Bere. Continue to climb gently and, at the brow of the hill, you reach a stile on the right.

2 Cross the stile signposted to the RIGHT. Walk in the direction indicated, climbing diagonally up the field towards a waymark post. Continue, still climbing, to the next waymark post. *You will soon enjoy a wide and splendid view over the Dysynni Valley, with the summit of Bird's Rock visible to the south-west.* Ignore a distinct track which curves to the right but continue ahead, passing to the left of a small clump of trees to find a well-hidden waymark post behind them. Follow the direction indicated, walking gently downhill and looking for a waymarked gate to the RIGHT. Cross a tiny stream, go through the gate and turn LEFT, to walk beside a wall. Continue with the wall on your left to pass a waymark post which indicates that you veer slightly to the right, but still keeping fairly close to the wall. Go through the gate ahead and immediately climb the waymarked stile. Now follow the path downhill, with Castell y Bere clearly visible ahead. As you pass to the left of a gorse bush the path splits – veer LEFT and continue downhill to join a green track. Continue ahead, looking out for a kissing-gate on the LEFT. Go through this and walk half-RIGHT towards a waymark post. Cross the stile by the post to join a road and turn RIGHT. You soon pass the entrance to Castell y Bere on the left, and the ruins are

WALK 10

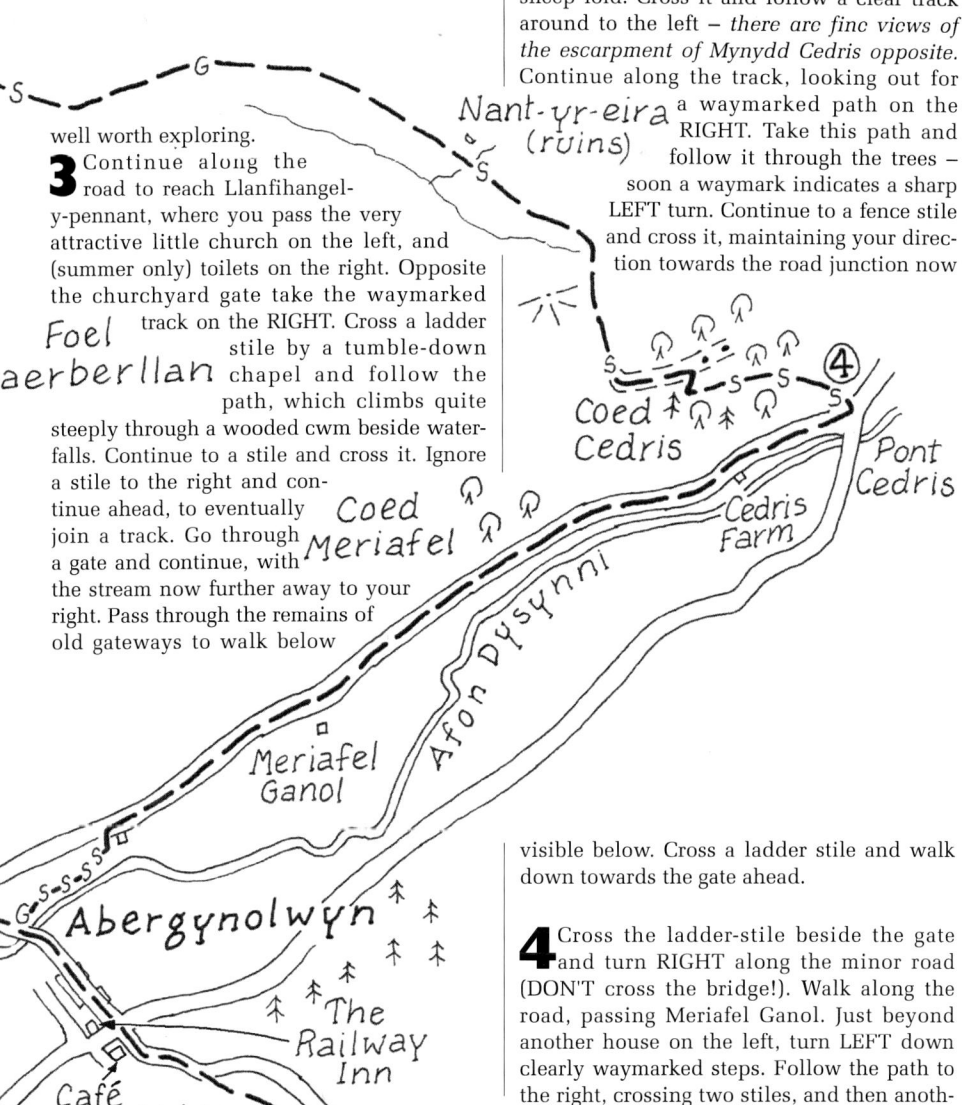

well worth exploring.

3 Continue along the road to reach Llanfihangel-y-pennant, where you pass the very attractive little church on the left, and (summer only) toilets on the right. Opposite the churchyard gate take the waymarked track on the RIGHT. Cross a ladder stile by a tumble-down chapel and follow the path, which climbs quite steeply through a wooded cwm beside waterfalls. Continue to a stile and cross it. Ignore a stile to the right and continue ahead, to eventually join a track. Go through a gate and continue, with the stream now further away to your right. Pass through the remains of old gateways to walk below the ruins of Nant-yr-eira, where you have to step across a stream to reach a ladder-stile by a gate. Cross it and continue, following the track. When a wall appears ahead veer to the RIGHT to reach a ladder-stile beside a sheep fold. Cross it and follow a clear track around to the left – *there are fine views of the escarpment of Mynydd Cedris opposite*. Continue along the track, looking out for a waymarked path on the RIGHT. Take this path and follow it through the trees – soon a waymark indicates a sharp LEFT turn. Continue to a fence stile and cross it, maintaining your direction towards the road junction now visible below. Cross a ladder stile and walk down towards the gate ahead.

4 Cross the ladder-stile beside the gate and turn RIGHT along the minor road (DON'T cross the bridge!). Walk along the road, passing Meriafel Ganol. Just beyond another house on the left, turn LEFT down clearly waymarked steps. Follow the path to the right, crossing two stiles, and then another by an old gate and continue half-right. Cross one more stile and walk with the river to your left. Rejoin the road at a kissing-gate by the bridge and turn left to return to Caffi'r Ceunant, The Railway Inn and Nant Gwernol Station.

Castell y Bere *See next page*

Castell y Bere

In one of the most romantic settings imaginable, where what was once the Dysinni estuary touches the foothills of the mighty Cadair Idris, this 13th century native Welsh castle seems almost to grow from the island of rock upon which it stands. Evidence of pre-medieval occupation has been found, but it was Llywelyn ap Iorwerth (the Great) who in 1221 regained control of Meirionnydd from Gryffydd, his son, and who began building here.

Llywelyn had always accepted that he should pay homage to the King of England, but claimed that his status should be equal to that of the King of Scots, and that the Welsh barons should pay homage to him, and not to the English King. This resulted in a strained relationship between the two rulers, although this was ameliorated for a while when Llywelyn married Joan, King John's illegitimate daughter, in 1205. Llywelyn was defeated by the English king in 1211, and died in 1240.

The castle was besieged by the English army under Edward I's Lieutenant, the Savoyard Sir Otto de Grandison, and fell on 25th April 1283, to be subsequently occupied by a few soldiers, carpenters and stonemasons. Edward intended to maintain Castell y Bere as a bastion of English power, and to found an English town and borough there. But none of this came to fruition, and the castle was re-captured by the Welsh in 1294, during Madog ap Llewelyn's revolt. Although the English expressed a desire to recapture it, the castle never again featured in the royal accounts, and subsequently fell into ruin.

The entrance was on the western side, defended by a draw-bridge and overlooked by a small tower. Just inside was a well, a vital asset for a building which was subject to siege. The middle tower was probably the main defensive structure, with another to the south containing living accommodation and the latrine.

Llanfihangel-y-pennant

In the village there is a monument to Mary Jones who, in 1804, walked over 50 miles barefoot to Bala to buy a bible. Unfortunately Thomas Charles had no bibles left, but he took pity on Mary and gave her his own copy. He then went on to found the British and Foreign Bible Society. His grandson, David Charles, founded Coleg y Bala in 1837. A statue of Thomas Charles can be seen in Bala.

Castell y Bere

WALK 11

DOLGOCH FALLS

DESCRIPTION From the station, follow the signs and the route given on this map. It is a splendid walk up one side to the upper falls, then across the bridge to return through the woods on the southern bank. Bear in mind that there are quite a few steep steps, and that they are often damp and a little slippery, so please TAKE CARE.

START Dolgoch Station

The path winds up the hillside from the first cascade passing through scrubby oak woodland, typical of rocky stream banks in Wales. Listen and watch here for pied flycatchers, redstarts and other woodland birds. There is a viewpoint and a bridge at the second set of falls, with a nearby fenced-off old mine shaft, one of many in this area. See how the shady conditions around the opening encourage canopies of ferns, with ivy and honeysuckle.

As you continue upstream, the path becomes more gentle with moss covered rocks lining the banks. Dippers are residents here, bobbing on the rocks and stoney edges. You soon come upon another bridge. If you have time, carry on along the path as it winds up away from the stream. The woodland changes in character, becoming more open, with hazel coppice and mountain ash (rowan). Bracken covered hillsides with bracken and hawthorn scrub, referred to as 'ffridd', which replace the oaks in these areas, are surprisingly rich in bird and other wildlife.

Back at the bridge, cross over at the upper falls (Pistyll Arian) and head downstream. This side of the watercourse is quite different, the slope being more gentle and the soil deeper. As a result the trees are taller and more stately, with lush undergrowth. Where streams trickle down the bank, flushes of moisture-loving plants occur, such as fluffy white flowered meadowsweet and low growing golden saxifrage.

Another small bridge across the stream by the viaduct brings you back onto your outward route. Noticeable on the wet rocks along this path are the succulent primitive green plants called liverworts, while on the drier grassy path-sides cow wheat, with long pale yellow flowers in July and August, grows.

We are pleased to acknowledge the help of the Royal Society for the Protection of Birds, who supplied this information.

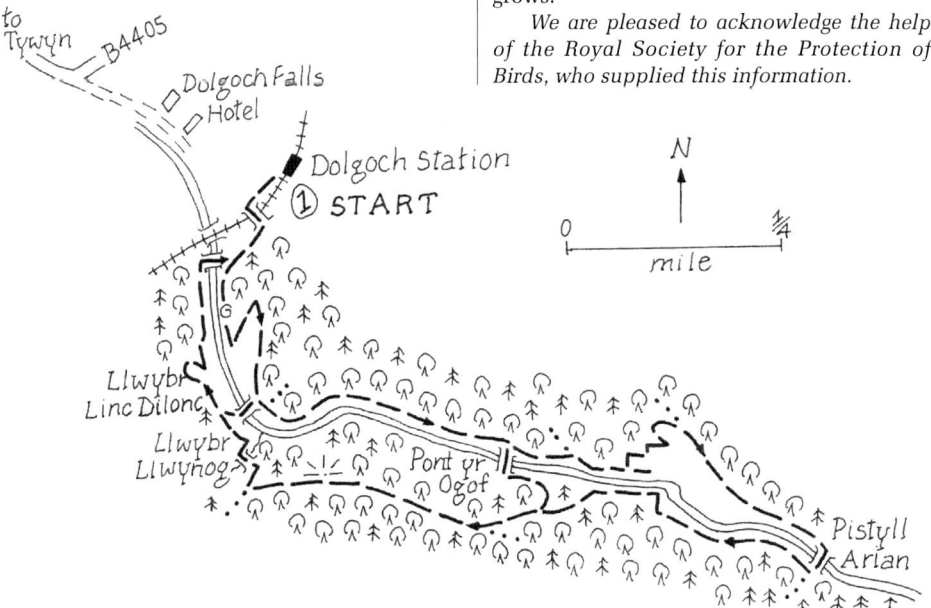

WALK 12
AROUND CYNFAL FARM

DESCRIPTION There is a choice of three stations to choose as the starting point. Fachgoch Halt is OK for those who do not mind climbing down from the carriage, since there is no platform – there is just a station nameplate here. Cynfal Halt has no station buildings, but it does have a basic small platform. Rhydyronen Station is more substantial, with a shelter and seats. This walk passes all three, so you can choose your starting point, or incorporate a short train ride into this 2½ mile walk, and make it even shorter. All the paths are clear, although it's fairly rough between briach-yn-rhiw and Bryn-y-castell, where you pass an ancient motte – a mound which was once topped with a wooden or stone 'castle'. There are excellent views to the east, north and west from many of the paths. Allow 2 hours for a leisurely outing.
START Either Fach-goch Halt, Cynfal Halt or Rhydyronen Station. Our description starts and ends at the latter.

1 Leave the station along the track, go through the gate and turn sharp RIGHT, crossing the bridge over the railway. When the road bends to the left, continue ahead through a gate. Carry on along the clear tarmac track. When the track splits, take the left hand fork, gently climbing. *Turn around occasionally to enjoy the splendid view.* Go through a metal gate and continue. When you reach the buildings, you come to two gateways – take the RIGHT-HAND one as waymarked. Go left to walk in front of farm buildings, then turn RIGHT through a metal gate at the corner.

2 Go through another gate and turn sharp RIGHT to walk along a green track behind the buildings you have just passed. Continue, looking for a stile ahead in the right-hand corner. Cross this and carry on, ducking under trees and with a fence about 5 yards to your right. *The mound of the motte, barely distinguishable, is up to your left.* Bryn-y-castell appears down to your right, and soon the path descends towards it. Finally you need to scramble down a small bank (take care) to join the farm track. Turn LEFT and carry on. *There is a very fine view to your right, over Broad Water (see Walk 2) and Cardigan Bay.*

3 Soon look for a waymarked walkers' gate down to your RIGHT. Cross a small stream and go through this gate, and follow the direction indicated by the waymark. Walk down the field and after about 100 yards look for a ladder-stile in a dip to your left, beyond a small stream, which you cross on stones. Climb the stile over the fence and carry on, veering slightly right. Cross a stile with a yellow-topped post beside it and carry on to a metal field gate, by large farm buildings. Go through the gate. Veer left, cross the end of the field to a tiny metal walkers' gate in the corner (it is quite well hidden!). Go though this and continue across the field towards the left-hand side of the buildings of Fach-goch. Go though the metal gate (you may have to climb this), turn RIGHT and walk on a rough track beside the buildings to a gate on the RIGHT.

4 Go though this gate and follow the track as it turns left between buildings. Go through a second gate, cross a track and carry on over the field downhill to a stile, *enjoying the view over Cardigan Bay.* Cross this stile and carry on. Soon the Talyllyn Railway comes into view. Turn RIGHT to walk with the line to your left, soon negotiating a very muddy patch. Go though a metal field gate and continue, passing what little comprises Fach-goch halt – just a crossing and a sign. Carry on, going through a gate to eventually come to gates either side of the road by Cynfal Halt, which you can access by a stile on your left. Continue ahead, crossing a stile

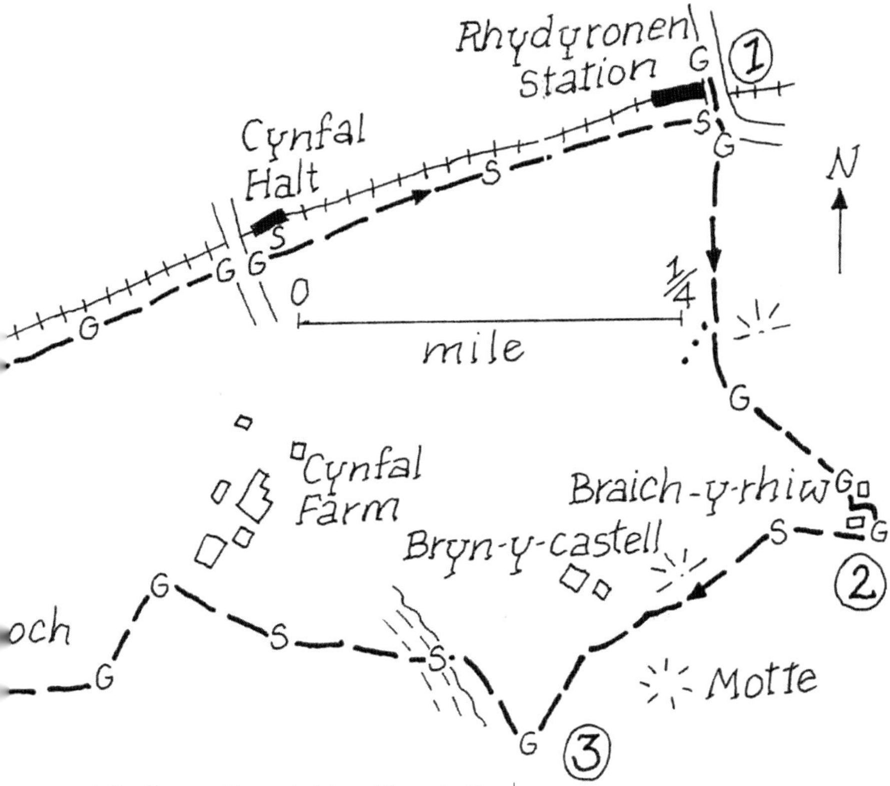

WALK 12

and finally reaching a ladder stile onto the road by Rhydyronen Station. Turn LEFT to return to the start.

Rhydyronen Station

WALK 13
WHARF STATION TO ABERDYFI

DESCRIPTION This is an easy 4 mile walk, where Tywyn and its caravans are soon left behind as you cross sandy pasture to approach Aberdyfi golf course. You then cross to the beach or dunes to enjoy the company of the sea. There are fine views to the hills inland and, when you reach Aberdyfi, you can visit this popular seaside resort. Allow 2 hours
START Wharf Station.
RETURN By train to Tywyn Station (www.thetrainline.com) or by X29 bus (www.lloydscoaches.com). Check the timetables – unless you choose to walk back.

1 Leave Wharf Station, walk over the bridge over the Cambrian Coast railway and continue along Neptune Road. Continue straight ahead at the junction with Warwick Place, staying on Neptune Road. Take the first LEFT towards Penllyn Caravan Park, walking towards a white house. Follow the track when it turns right, go though a gate and continue ahead, going through two more gates and following the the rough tarmac track as it bends left, eventually leaving the caravans behind. You reach another gate, and go through.

2 Carry on ahead to another gate, which you go through and then on to another. The track becomes quite faint now, and swings gently to the right to pass a small lake on the left. Continue ahead to approach the golf course. Now look out for a stile on the right.

3 Cross this stile and turn LEFT. You now have a choice: maintain your direction and either follow a path along the top of the dunes following the white posts (essential if your walk coincides with a high spring tide) or descend to the beach to walk along the sand (probably easier). Gradually your route swings left.

4 Look out for a diamond-shaped yellow sign on a post in the dunes. About 25 yards beyond this cross the dunes to reach

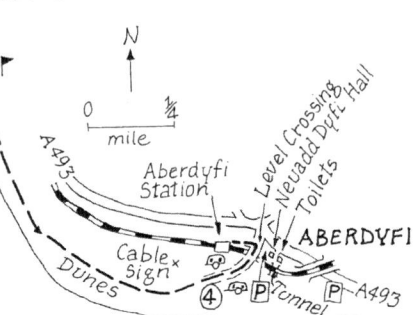

a caravan park. Walk through the park, veering right, to reach a toilet block (private) and turn left to a level crossing. CAREFULLY cross the line – stop, look, listen – then turn LEFT to reach Aberdyfi Station for a train back to Tywyn. If you wish to visit Aberdyfi, continue ahead from the crossing and turn right at the main road (passing public toilets). You can walk back to Tywyn by returning along the beach, and then continuing straight ahead at point 3.

WALKS 13 & 14

WALK 14
NORTH TO TONFANAU

DESCRIPTION An easy, level, 3 mile walk north out of Tywyn with some excellent views of the surrounding hills, including Birds' Rock. You then pass Broad Water to cross the Afon Dysynni on the handsome new foot and cycle bridge. It's then an easy stroll to Tonfanau Station.

START Wharf Station, Tywyn.

RETURN By train to Tywyn Station (www.thetrainline.com) Check the timetables – unless you choose to walk back. You can do this by returning to cross the footbridge then staying on the road back to Tywyn, which is quicker than following the outward route (but it's dull!)

From Wharf Station walk to the A493 Station Road and turn LEFT to continue towards the town centre, passing Tywyn Station. When the road turns sharply right by the railway bridge you carry on virtually straight across into Idris Villas. Walk along this road – *over to right is the 15 acre Novus Solar Farm, opened in 2016. It is capable of generating 2.8 megawatts, enough to meet the needs of about 750 homes.* Carry on along what is now Sandilands Road, passing Morfa Camp on the right – once a base for the Royal Artillery anti-aircraft practice camp at Tonfanau. When you approach a level crossing, don't cross it, but turn RIGHT and continue, passing houses on the right beyond a wide grass verge, with the railway on the left. Pass the first turning on the right and carry on.

2 Turn RIGHT just before the speed de-restriction signs, following the direction indicated by the waymark sign, to walk along a rough road. Go through the small pedestrian gate to the right of wider gates and then veer around to the LEFT following the track, which swings right then left, *passing old concrete foundations, dating from the area's old military days.* Carry on ahead, *enjoying very fine panoramic views to the right, with Birds' Rock being prominent in the centre.* Pass an old low pill-box, linked to an underground air-raid shelter, on the left. Turn LEFT at the T junction of tracks then immediately swing RIGHT to cross a bridge, with gates at either end, over a drainage channel. Climb a small embankment and carry on, veering slightly left towards the new white-arched footbridge in the distance. The path is not at all clear, but if you keep heading towards the footbridge you will be fine. You may have to skirt a marshy area in the centre. *To your right is the expanse of Broad Water, a tidal lake which becomes an expanse of mainly sand at low water.*

3 As you approach the Afon Dysynni to your right you go though a gate, which is soon followed by another gate onto the road. Turn RIGHT and cross the new foot and cycle bridge. *Families enjoy visiting the river here for a spot of gentle canoeing, or a paddle.* Follow the narrow tarmac road which swings around to the left to run parallel to the railway. Continue until you are faced with metal gates. Here you turn sharp RIGHT to join the road, where you turn LEFT then continue to Tonfanau Station. Here you can catch a train (request stop) to return to Tywyn Station. It is then just a short walk back to Wharf Station.

WALK 15
THE TONFANAU LOOP

DESCRIPTION Navigation is easy on this gentle walk, which starts and finishes on a very quiet minor road by the railway, then soon veers away, passing some remains of the old army camp, which existed here. A sharp turn south takes you along an old bridleway which climbs very gently to give you fine coastal views. Some handsome farm houses are passed before you reach Tonfanau Quarry, where you make a short descent back to the very quiet road. Tonfanau means ' Place of the Waves'. The route is about 3½ miles, and you should allow about 2 hours.

START Take the train from Tywyn Station (Cambrian Coast) to Tonfanau. Make sure you mention to the guard that you wish to get off at Tonfanau – it's a request stop. Tywyn Station is a 5 minute walk from Wharf Station.

1 From the platform, cross the level crossing to the road. *By the widened entrance area is a plaque mounted on a stone, dedicated to the All Arms Junior Leaders Regiment who occupied the camp here between 1959-66. Inside the gates are buildings surviving from that time, part of which are used as the base for the 1 mile Tonfanau Race Circuit, where there are four motor cycle events each year (www.tonfanauroadracing.co.uk).* and turn LEFT to follow the road, which soon swings to the right. *The seashore is to your left where, out of sight, is a row of old practice gun emplacements.* Continue along the road, passing a strange structure on the left. *This is the old 25 yard rifle range – time has taken its toll, and the building associated with this has gone, leaving only the foundation. The views over Cardigan Bay are good.* Continue along the road, passing the buildings of Llanfendigaid. *This estate has been owned by the Nanney-Wynn family since AD 1241. Originally the estate occupied an area stretching from Harlech in the north to Aberystwyth in the south. Now reduced in size, it provides luxury self-catering holiday accommodation in buildings with listed status. There is a heated indoor swimming pool. Llanfendigaid Farm adjoins.* Carry on to reach Bwlch on the left, with the converted Capel y Bwlch opposite.

2 Immediately after the chapel turn sharp RIGHT to walk up a grassy bridleway. Continue to pass through a gate at Tyddyn Meurig, then look for a concrete step on the left. Step up and veer right to go through a waymarked gate. Carry on to soon pass through another gate, still climbing gently with a fence to the right and a steep slope to the left. Go through a wooden gate, pass just above Bronclydwr and walk to another gate. *There are excellent views over the coast here.* Go through this gate and begin a gradual descent.

3 The path bends left to go through a wooden gate to approach Cefncamberth. A flurry of gates take you behind the buildings. When the path splits into three, take the middle option. You walk by a handsome little 'well' building on the left. Go through a gate and carry on. You pass a dried up reservoir on the left to reach a little metal gate. Go through and climb up a rocky path to emerge between gorse bushes and reach a prominent yellow waymark post indicating the Wales Coast Path. Carry on ahead as indicated to start descending through the edge of the quarry. You reach a cleared area where an old excavating machine stands decaying. Turn RIGHT to walk to the right along a wider track and below a large cylindrical rusting tank. *The Dysinni Bridge and the splendid new footbridge come into distant view.* Continue down the track, passing old quarry ponds and ruined buildings up to the left, and past a square control room building. *A look through the window reveals a large switch panel and other items, all in remarkably good order, although obviously disused.* Carry on down to the chained-up metal gates.

4 Walk though the gap to the right of the gates, by a waymark post, turn RIGHT along the road, enjoying the view, to walk back to the station. *The road here was once a railway branch line which served the quarry,*

WALK 15

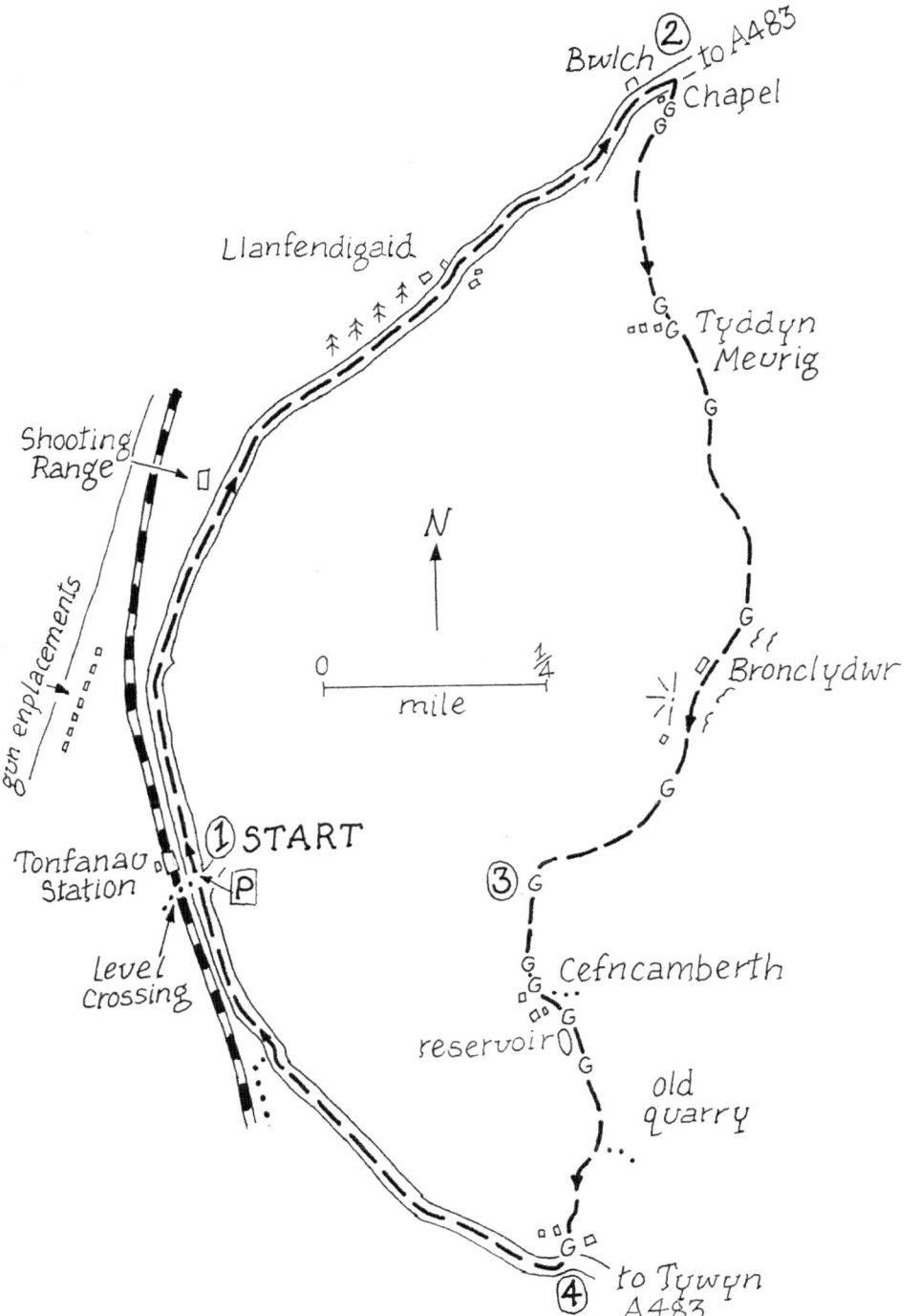

WALK 16
ALLTWYLLT INCLINE

DESCRIPTION This is an easy walk, but with one or two fairly steep sections. Having crossed the Nant Gwernol Footbridge you walk alongside a series of very attractive waterfalls on the Nant Gwernol. You then cross another footbridge to return along what was once the trackbed of the railway from Bryn-Eglwys Quarry. Soon you arrive at the top of the Alltwyllt Incline, where wagons were raised and lowered to the railway below. Steps bring you back to the station. 1½ miles, 1½ hours.
START Nant Gwernol Station.

The top of the Alltwyllt Incline is marked by the two walls of an old stable and, if you look above you to the left, the old winding house. Small sections of track reveal the top of the incline, where trucks loaded with slate were lowered, using the cable to raise the empty trucks from the bottom, where the loaded wagons were then steam hauled to the Cambrian Railway for transportation to the harbour at Aberdyfi.

*Q*uarrying was begun at Bryn Eglwys in the 1840s by John Pughe of Aberdyfi, with the slate being transported by cart and pack horse to Aberdyfi. The quarry was leased in 1864 by William McConnel, an English cotton mill owner. Being situated 430 feet above Nant Gwernol Station, horse-drawn tramways and the Cantrebedd and Beudynewydd inclines made getting the slate off the mountain an arduous task.

It was this laborious transportation to the coast which was holding back profitability. His solution was to build the Talyllyn Railway. Even with this the quarry still struggled to survive, and it was placed for auction in 1879. There was little interest, and finally McConnel bought the quarry himself – just as the slate market began to boom. He finally made a short-lived profit before his death in 1902. Henry Haydn Jones, a Welsh Liberal, bought the quarry, along with the railway, and production again began, continuing until 1946, when a collapse finally brought about its closure.

Leave the far end of the platform at Nant Gwernol Station and walk ahead, ignoring steps which come in from the right – this is your return route. Continue ahead, then turn LEFT to cross the river on the footbridge. Turn RIGHT and continue with the river on your right. *This is a very attractive stretch, with numerous waterfalls and pools.* When you reach a second footbridge turn RIGHT to cross the river, climb up to reach a path where you turn RIGHT. *You are now walking along the trackbed of the Galltymoelfre horse-drawn tramway, with the river down to the right.* Follow the path beside the top of the incline then zig-zag down to prominent steps which take you down to the station. A short flight of stone steps completes the return to the start.

WALK 17
ABERGYNOLWYN – NANT GWERNOL LINK

DESCRIPTION The route between Abergynolwyn Station and Nant Gwernol Station (red waymarks) takes you beside the railway and through some very attractive woodland, making it really more than just a link route. It combines very well with a continuation down to the village beside a series of falls and pools on the Nnat Gwernol, in the midst of shady woodland. You can then reward yourself with either a pint and/or a meal at The Railway Inn (friendly, real ale, good food, 01654 782744) or a meal at the excellent and friendly Caffi'r Ceunant (01654 782372, 09.00-16.00, closed Tuesday). If you would like to make this a round trip, there is a footway alongside the road to Abergynolwyn Station, and although it is OK it is not particularly interesting. Or you can walk uphill back to Nant Gwernol Station, assuming you have checked the train times and have the correct tickets! Remember that if you are using the train and walking station to station here, you must have valid tickets for your journey

From Abergynolwyn Station walk down the approach road, looking for a signed footpath, up steps, on the right. Turn RIGHT and follow the path uphill towards the railway. Follow the obvious path beside the track, with a very fine slate and wire fence to your right, passing and ignoring a pedestrian tunnel under the railway. Negotiate steps down and then up to cross over a stream and continue, with the path ducking and weaving, to eventually climb steps to reach a narrow road at an ungated level crossing. Turn sharp RIGHT to carefully cross the railway and follow the road, which soon becomes an unsurfaced track, to reach a wide T junction at a large sign. Turn LEFT here to walk gently uphill through attractive mixed woodland, soon catching glimpses of Abergynolwyn down on the left. You pass a waterfall and eventually the track veers right and ends at a turning point. Continue ahead, now along a path, until you reach a fork. Go LEFT and zig-zag downhill to Nant Gwernol station.

To continue to Abergynolwyn turn RIGHT and follow the path over the river bridge. Turn LEFT to walk beside the tumbling waters and eventually join the road down to

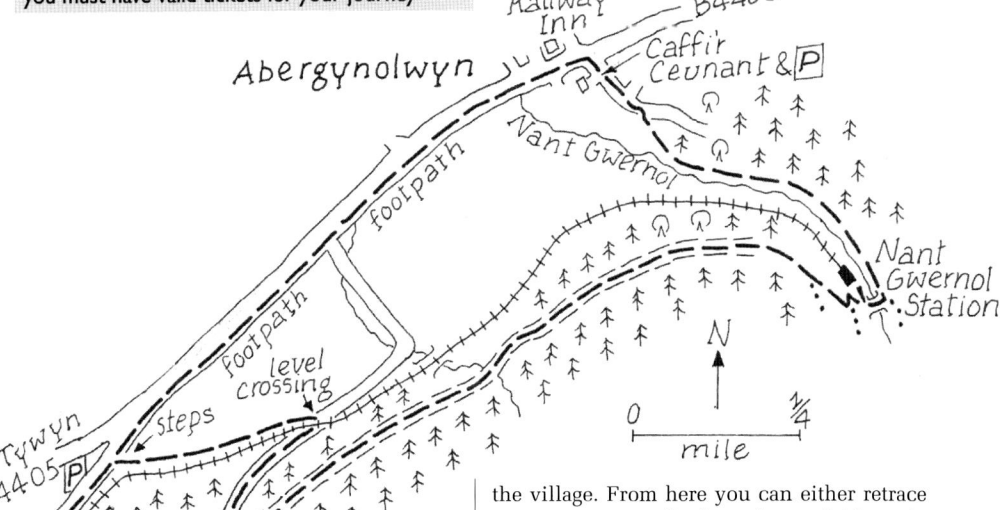

the village. From here you can either retrace your steps, or walk along the roadside path, back to the station, for a circular walk..

WALK 18
BRYN EGLWYS QUARRY

DESCRIPTION Although quite short, this is a very demanding walk, where you spend the first half climbing some steep paths and steps to reach the disused quarry, which is situated near the head of a very beautiful cwm. Fortunately the route is easily followed, and you can make plenty of stops to enjoy excellent views. Some stretches pass through a rich mixture of woodland, with a variety of native trees, along with some handsome tall pines. For much of your walk you will be accompanied by the sound of tumbling water and waterfalls, and should you enjoy industrial archaeology, there are tantalising remains. The walk is about 4 miles long, and you need to allow about 3 hours to complete it. Add about ¾ of a mile there and back (including a steep hill) to visit the village.
START Nant Gwernol Station or, if you wish, Abergynolwyn village, where there is a really excellent café, serving some imaginative dishes along with the usual fare, and an attractive pub.

1 From the end of the platform follow the path beside the river to cross the Nant Gwernol Footbridge *(opened by Lord Parry in 1980)*. Climb steps to follow the path, with the river to your right. *Take time to enjoy the waterfalls and pools.* You pass a signboard, with a footbridge over to your right. Climb steps and continue along the path, which eventually swings left away from the river, zig-zags up steps and passes a waymark post to reach a gate at the top.

2 Go through the gate and turn RIGHT. Pass a gate and stile on the right and continue. You come to a vehicle track which leaves the right – DON'T follow this but do follow the waymarked green track between this and the track you have just left. Continue, soon catching sight of stone spoil heaps across the valley to your right, and soon also ahead. Pass a large isolated gatepost on the left as the track swings round to the right. Pass a small waterfall to your left, and some quite dramatic heaps of large stones to reach a gate, which you go through. You pass between some attractive woodlands and a very deep and dangerous quarry on your left, beyond a fence. DO NOT approach this quarry.

3 You come to a metal gate and a stile – the fence however is trodden down to the left so you can easily walk by. Pass a yellow-topped post with a waymark (ignore this one), immediately followed by a shorter post with a blue waymark. You reach a clearing where vehicles can turn – look over to the left to find a blue waymark on a post by a 'wind-up' recording on a sturdy post close by. *There are a couple more of these on this route and it is well worth following the instructions to hear about the history of the quarry and the men who worked here (in Welsh or English).* Go though the open gap in the fence and continue, along a narrow path, which winds through attractive woodland. The path is a little faint in places but if you look carefully you won't lose it. It climbs gently to a fence, then much more steeply beside it, alongside spoil heaps and eventually old quarry workings. You pass between the scant remains of old quarry buildings and eventually leave the fence to climb a slope to pass between tumbling walls. At the top you pass what looks like an old entrance. The path zig-zags and then swings to the right, and here you begin your descent. At the bottom of the slope you come to another 'recording winder'. Continue along the track ahead – *through trees on the right are further remains of quarrying.*

WALK 18

4 When you reach a substantial track which crosses, look ahead for a blue waymarked path, and follow this. It soon becomes a clear track and continues descending, initially between a forest plantation, and then mixed woodland. There are remains of an old building on the left. You descend to a tumbling stream which you cross using a footbridge, then turn RIGHT. You descend, often using steps, between tall conifers to follow the stream, passing the footbridge seen on your outward journey. On your way back to the station you will pass some old discarded sections of track and partially buried sleepers to eventually reach the top of the Allt Wyllt Incline. The path here descends beside a handrail and a long flight of steps back down to the station.

*T*he top of the Alltwyllt Incline is marked by the two walls of an old stable and, if you look above you to the left, the old drum house. Small sections of track reveal the top of the incline, where trucks loaded with slate were lowered, using a cable to raise the empty trucks from the bottom. A brake-man controlled their descent (not always successfully!). The rest of the time, on the level, the trucks were pulled by horses. The loaded wagons were then steam hauled to the Cambrian Railway for transportation to the harbour at Aberdyfi.

*Q*uarrying was begun at Bryn Eglwys in the 1840s by John Pughe of Aberdyfi, with the slate being transported by cart and pack horse to Aberdyfi. The quarry was leased in 1864 by William McConnel, an English cotton mill owner. Being situated 430 feet above Nant Gwernol Station, horse-drawn tramways and the Cantrebedd and Beudynewydd inclines made getting the slate off the mountain a laborious and difficult task. All the quarrying was underground, where the slate was blasted along existing fault lines. The quarrymen often worked suspended by chains, with the only light from candles. The slate was split into slabs and hoisted to the surface using power from a waterwheel. Trucks were pulled by horses, a very inefficient means of distribution. His solution was to build the Talyllyn Railway. With this the quarry still struggled to survive, and it was placed for auction in 1879. There was little interest, and finally McConnel bought the quarry himself – just as the slate market began to boom. He eventually made a short-lived profit before his death in 1902. Henry Haydn Jones, a Welsh Liberal, purchased the quarry, along with the railway, and production again began, continuing until 1946 when a collapse finally brought about its closure.

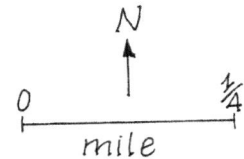

WALK 19
ALL AROUND TYWYN

DESCRIPTION On the face of it, this looks like a town walk but, when you have completed it, you will have seen hills, fields and coastal flatlands along with aspects of Tywyn which are really very attractive. You can include a visit to the church. It is short, so it makes a great outing for a sunny evening, or you could stop off at Pendre Station if you have been walking further up the line, and return to Wharf Station via Leahurst for an additional stroll. There are no hills and route finding is easy whether you are walking clockwise or anti-clockwise.
START Wharf Station or Pendre Station.

1 Leave Wharf Station, walk over the bridge over the main line railway and and continue along Neptune Road. Continue straight ahead at the junction with Warwick Place, staying on Neptune Road. Take the first LEFT towards Penllyn Caravan Park, walking towards a white house. Follow the track when it turns RIGHT, go though a gate and then turn LEFT as waymarked to go through a second gate and head across a field to another gate. Go though and walk diagonally across the field to reach a wooden gate by a red-brick house.

2 Go through the gate. Continue ahead then turn left and carry on to the first road on the right. Turn RIGHT here and then RIGHT again passing the house with the track of a model railway going all around it. Take the first LEFT and carry on to reach a rough green path which soon brings you to a small gate. Go through. Continue with a little ditch on the right to another little metal gate, which you go through. Walk beside a ditch to yet another gate and go through, then carry on to reach a gate by the railway.

3 Go though and CAREFULLY cross the track. LOOK & LISTEN FOR TRAINS APPROACHING. TAKE CARE. Go though a second gate and carry on along the wide rough path with caravans to your right. Pass the large barn on the left and turn LEFT to walk through a gateway. Walk ahead. The track soon become grassy with hedgerows either side. When you join a tarmac access road carry on ahead to join the main road opposite Pant y Neuadd Caravan Park.

4 Turn RIGHT and walk along the main road on a wide verge. Pass Carreg Lwyd on the left and continue. Look out for a footpath sign on the opposite side. Turn LEFT here, carefully cross the road and climb steps to follow a path, with a fence on the right. Go through a small metal gate and carry on ahead, with the fence on your right. Go through another small metal gate, veer left to another small gate, go through and join a road.

5 Turn LEFT and walk along the road until you reach the crossroads by the entrance to Ty Mawr. Here you turn LEFT and walk along the road between fields, with the tower of St Cadfan's church ahead. When you join houses on the left, carry on AHEAD to cross the level crossing at Pendre Station. Pass a little public garden on the right, and follow the road around to the right and carry straight on to reach the entrance to the church.

6 Turn LEFT to walk along the main road, passing the old Market Hall clock tower on the right, built to celebrate Queen Victoria's Diamond Jubilee in 1897 and which now houses the Salt Marsh Café Bar, and shops and cafés. Follow the road around to the left when you reach Tywyn Station, with the railway bridge ahead, and carry on passing the school to return to Wharf Station and the Talyllyn Railway.

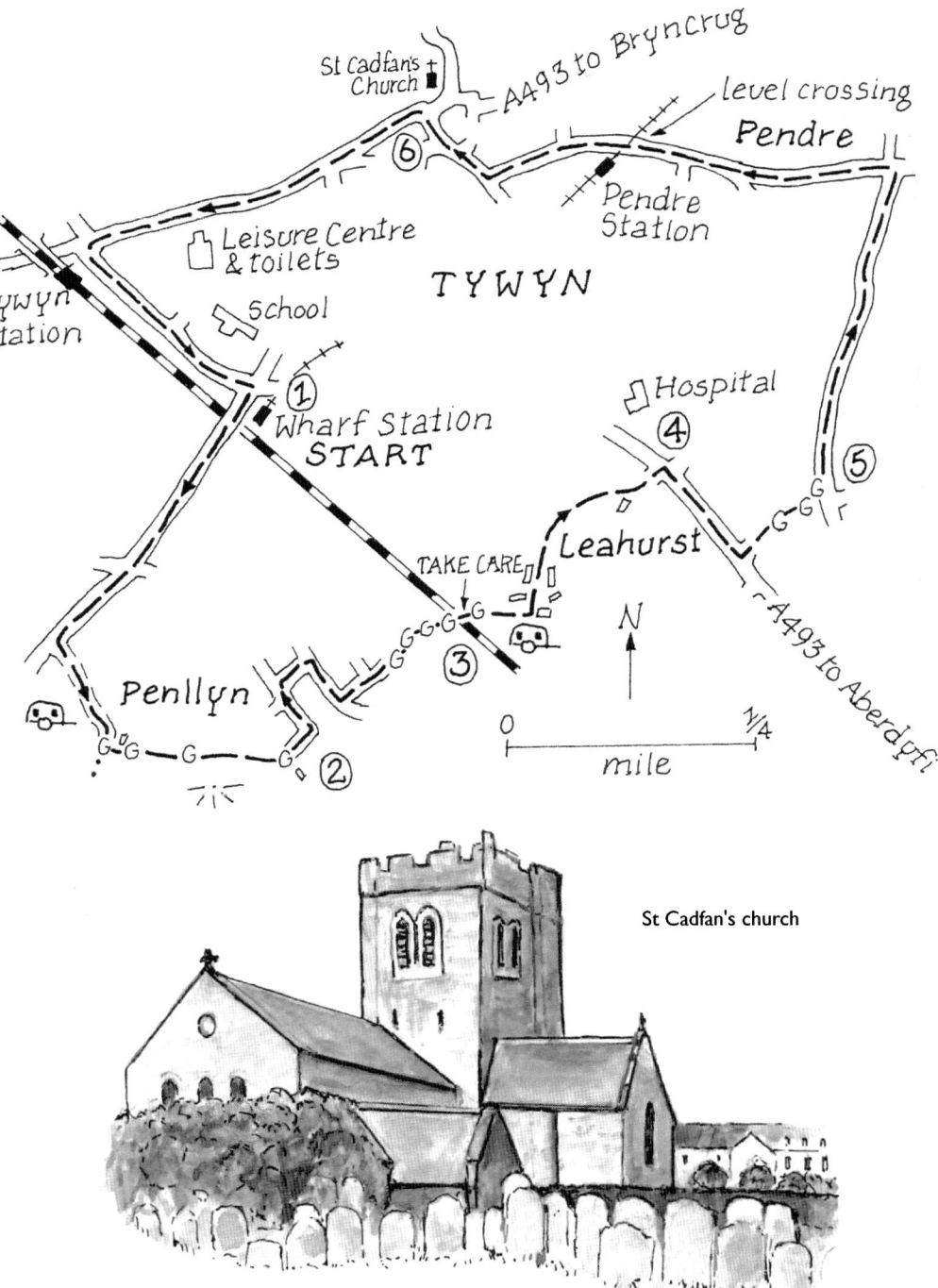

St Cadfan's church

WALK 20
A TRAIN, A BUS & A LAKE

DESCRIPTION Beyond Abergynolwyn, nestled between dramatic and steep mountainsides lies Tal-y-llyn Lake, a beautiful expanse of quite shallow water on the Bala fault line, where the average depth is only about 10 ft. Immediately to the north is Cadair Idris, while to the south the slopes are crowned by the rough crags of Graig Goch. The view to the north-east, along the valley, is truly stunning. Technically Tal-y-llyn is a glacial ribbon lake, formed from a glacial trough once the ice had melted. A landslip then dammed the water. If you enjoy local fiction, the lake features in 'The Grey King', a fantasy novel by Susan Cooper published in 1976. The lake's name has an interesting translation – being literally 'the lake at the end of the lake'. Its Welsh name is Llyn Mwyngll, relating to its narrow profile. Route finding on the actual walk is easy, and so is the going underfoot. But you must plan your visit to avoid a walk alongside, albeit light, traffic!

START To visit this wonderful place will require a day put aside, and a touch of expeditionary spirit. *During the summer, when there are plenty of trains running on the Talyllyn, and you would like to travel by train and bus (route 30), you will need catch a train to Abergynolwyn around 10.30 to connect with a bus at around 11.19. Ask to travel to the far end of the lake. For the return from the Pen-y-bont Hotel at the southern end, you catch a bus around 13.38 to connect with a train at Abergynolwyn around 15.11. But YOU MUST CHECK THE TRAIN AND BUS TIMES*, as they can change, and there are NO BUSES ON SUNDAYS & RESTRICTED SERVICES ON BANK HOLIDAYS – www.talyllyn.co.uk/timetable for the train and www.lloydscoaches.com/Timetables for bus route 30. This arrangement will allow you 2 hours for the walk (which takes about an hour) plus a short picnic. If this all seems too complicated, or you are travelling off-season when there are fewer trains, you can do the whole journey to Talyllyn Lake, the far end, by bus (route 30) from High Street, Tywyn.

1 From the bus stop at the top end of the lake, maintain your direction for about 25 yards, pass a stone building and turn LEFT onto a footpath. Go through a metal pedestrian gate and continue. Walk confined between wire fences to come to a second small gate and a small footbridge. Go through the gate, cross the bridge and turn LEFT. Walk by the edge of the field, pass a gate on your left and carry on to a gate ahead and go through. This it marked by a yellow-topped post. Walk half RIGHT across the field to second yellow-topped post. The end of the lake comes into view to your left. The course of the path soon becomes apparent in the grass. You cross a narrow footbridge by the post, cross a stile and swing LEFT just after a tree to follow the narrow path marked by a post. Reach a footbridge over a ditch, cross this and go through a small metal gate and continue ahead as waymarked. *There are great views of the mountains and the lake from here.* Follow the narrow path to reach a footbridge over the Afon Faw, full of small fish in the spring. Cross the bridge but don't follow the track ahead – veer to the the LEFT to ascend gently and shortly join the rough road.

2 Turn LEFT and walk along this quiet road, enjoying splendid views over the lake as the road gently climbs. Go through a gate by Pentre Farm, an attractive building with stone barns, all at the bottom of a steep cwm and enclosed on three sides by trees, idyllic but sadly abandoned. Go through a second gate and carry on. The road now comes down to the lakeside, where there is a wonderful spot for a picnic, with the Ty'n-y-cornel Hotel in view on the far side. Approaching the end of the lake there is another fine picnic spot. Go through a gate below the handsome Old Rectory B&B

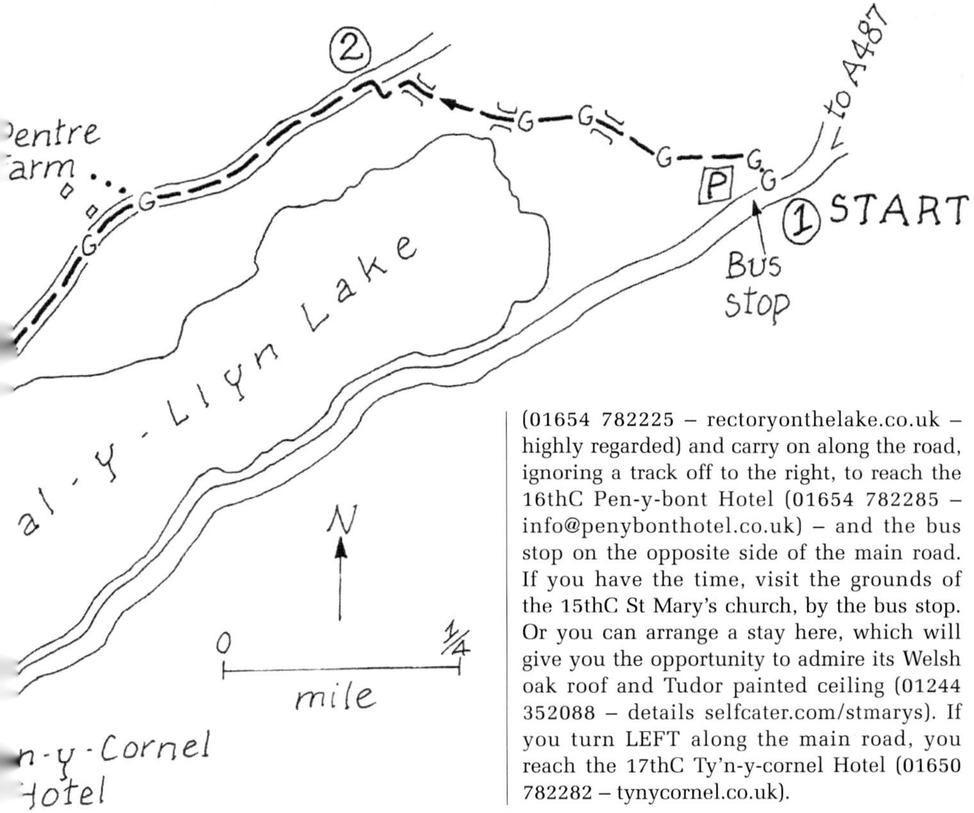

WALK 20

(01654 782225 – rectoryonthelake.co.uk – highly regarded) and carry on along the road, ignoring a track off to the right, to reach the 16thC Pen-y-bont Hotel (01654 782285 – info@penybonthotel.co.uk) – and the bus stop on the opposite side of the main road. If you have the time, visit the grounds of the 15thC St Mary's church, by the bus stop. Or you can arrange a stay here, which will give you the opportunity to admire its Welsh oak roof and Tudor painted ceiling (01244 352088 – details selfcater.com/stmarys). If you turn LEFT along the main road, you reach the 17thC Ty'n-y-cornel Hotel (01650 782282 – tynycornel.co.uk).

Ty'n-y-cornel Hotel

PRONUNCIATION

Welsh	English equivalent
c	always hard, as in **c**at
ch	as in the Scottish word lo**ch**
dd	as th in **th**en
f	as f in o**f**
ff	as ff in o**ff**
g	always hard as in **g**ot
ll	no real equivalent. It is like 'th' in then, but with an 'L' sound added to it, giving 'thlan' for the pronunciation of the Welsh 'Llan'.

In Welsh the accent usually falls on the last-but-one syllable of a word.

KEY TO THE MAPS

- ➔ Walk route and direction
- ─── Metalled road
- ─ ─ ─ Unsurfaced road
- • • • • Footpath/route adjoining walk route
- ∿ River/stream
- ⚘ Trees
- ▬▬ Railway
- **G** Gate
- **S** Stile
- **F.B.** Footbridge
- ⇡ Viewpoint
- **P** Parking

PHOTO CREDITS

Front cover: *Main: Dolgoch crossing Dolgoch Viaduct & inset: departing Dolgoch Station – both Darren Turner*
Back cover: *Museum – Kes Jones*
Nant Gwernol, Dolgoch sign, The Railway Inn – David Perrott
Inside front cover: *Top– Barbara Fuller*
Centre – David Perrott
Bottom: – Ralph Ward

THE COUNTRYSIDE CODE

- Be safe – plan ahead and follow any signs
- Leave gates and property as you find them
- Protect plants and animals, and take your litter home
- Keep dogs under close control
- Consider other people

Open Access
Some routes cross areas of land where walkers have the legal right of access under The CRoW Act 2000 introduced in May 2005. Access can be subject to restrictions and closure for land management or safety reasons for up to 28 days a year. Details from: www.naturalresourceswales.gov.uk.
Please respect any notices.

Published by **Kittiwake Books Limited**
3 Glantwymyn Village Workshops, Glantwymyn, Machynlleth, Montgomeryshire SY20 8LY

© Text & map research: David Perrott 2019
© Maps & drawings: Kittiwake Books Ltd 2019

Drawings by Morag Perrott

Care has been taken to be accurate. However neither the author, the publisher nor the Tal-y-llyn Railway can accept responsibility for any errors which may appear, or their consequences. If you are in any doubt about access, check before you proceed.
Printed by Mixam UK.
ISBN: **978 1 908748 59 1**